S0-CFT-611

VISION BEARERS

Dynamic Evangelism in the 21st Century

RICHARD KEW AND CYRIL OKOROCHA

Foreword by the Archbishop of Canterbury

MOREHOUSE PUBLISHING
Harrisburg, Pennsylvania

BV
3790
.K495
1996

*"This Conference, recognizing that evangelism is
the primary task given to the Church, asks each
Province and diocese of the Anglican Communion, in
cooperation with other Christians, to make the
closing years of this millennium a 'Decade of Evangelism'
with a renewed emphasis on making Christ known
to the people of his world."*

(Resolution 43 of the Lambeth Conference of Bishops, 1988)

We dedicate this book to all those who made the G-CODE 2000 Conference possible, and to all the faithful evangelists of the worldwide Anglican Communion.

We also dedicate this book to Sharing Our Ministries Abroad (SOMA), whose vision it was that a book like this should be written.

We dedicate this book to our loving wives.

◆ ◆ ◆ ◆ ◆

O God,
You have made of one blood all the peoples of the earth,
and sent your blessed Son to preach peace to those who are far off
and to those who are near:
Grant that people everywhere may seek after you and find you;
bring the nations into your fold;
pour out your Spirit upon all flesh;
and hasten the coming of your kingdom;
through Jesus Christ our Lord.
Amen

(From the *Book of Common Prayer of the Episcopal Church of the USA*, adapted from a prayer by George Edward Lynch Cotton, Bishop of Calcutta, 1850-1866)

Copyright © 1996 by Richard Kew and Cyril Okorocha

All rights reserved. No part of this book may be reproduced or transmitted in any form or by any means, electronic or mechanical, including photocopying, recording, or by any information storage and retrieval system, without written permission from the publisher.

MOREHOUSE PUBLISHING

Editorial Office:
871 Ethan Allen Highway
Ridgefield, CT 06877

Corporate Office:
PO Box 1321
Harrisburg, PA 17105

A catalog record for this book is available from the Library of Congress.
ISBN: 0-8192-1656-9

Printed in the United States of America

■ Contents

Foreword

The G-CODE 2000 Conference at Kanuga in September 1995 provided an invaluable opportunity for reflecting on the progress of the "Decade of Evangelism" throughout the Anglican Communion. Those who were there were left in no doubt that the Holy Spirit is doing remarkable things in many parts of the world at present.

Vision Bearers gives its readers a chance to appreciate something of the richness and wide diversity involved in evangelism and mission today. It is a seamless robe that includes pastoral care and social witness, as well as direct evangelistic outreach. I encourage all Anglicans to "read, study, learn and inwardly digest" the lessons that this book brings. It is inspiring, challenging and exciting and I warmly commend it to the Communion.

George Carey
Archbishop of Canterbury

Preface

The Global Conference for Dynamic Evangelism Beyond the Year 2000 is the somewhat unwieldy name given to a gathering of Anglican Christians from all over the world that took place at the Kanuga Conference Center, Hendersonville, NC, on September 4-9, 1995. It quickly became known as G-CODE 2000, for short. For a glorious late summer week high in the Great Smoky Mountains, delegates from 54 different countries met to listen, learn, pray, and dream about the evangelistic mission of the worldwide Anglican Communion as we enter the Third Millennium.

It was an extraordinary occasion, made all the more wonderful by the logistical barriers which were scaled to get people from lands where there is war, civil unrest, or political and religious discrimination against Christians, as well as women and men from countries, both very poor and incredibly affluent, from all over the globe. In words it is impossible to describe what it feels like to be part of such a "pentecostal" gathering.

The conference illustrated how much the center of gravity of the Anglican Communion has shifted from the wealthy global North to the poor, but spiritually vibrant, South. The worship and music illustrated the cultural and spiritual diversity of a worldwide church which was once, oh, so English! There seemed nothing incongruous about English or Canadian archbishops, clad in copes and mitres, swaying to the throb of African drums. On one occasion the worship even erupted into a spontaneous "liturgical conger!"

It was a privilege to be there. Cyril, in his role as Director of Evangelism and Mission of the Anglican Communion, had been behind this project from the beginning. For him, this was a dream come to fruition. Richard was there as a proverbial "fly on the wall," commissioned to observe the event and then to attempt to pull the diverse threads together to make this book. The opening day of the gathering was the first time we had ever met, but during the next ten days a firm friendship was forged which we are confident will last the rest of our lives! Perhaps it is fitting that such a global book be written by an African living in England, and an Englishman who long ago moved to the USA.

There are many people to thank who have helped us along our way, but special mention needs to be made of Edwina Thomas, Executive Director of SOMA-USA (Sharing Our Ministries Abroad), who first had the vision for this book. Over the years teams from SOMA have gone all over the world sharing skills and sharing the Good News, Edwina had seen a lot of the wonderful things going on in our worldwide church, and knew the story was a good one and needed to be told. We want to express particular gratitude to those who shared their stories with us. We also thank the staff of the Kanuga Conference Center, who gave us space to hatch the book, the staff of the Anglican Communion office in London, Allen Kelley and his colleagues at the Morehouse Publishing Company, and, of course, our long-suffering wives and children, whose prayers and input have helped make a far better end-product.

Vision Bearers was written in 14 weeks by two priests with busy travel schedules. It was composed in part in North Carolina, Tennessee, Russia, the Persian Gulf, California, various corners of England, and Washington State, to name but a few places! It is not a great work of literature, but neither is it intended to be an exhaustive study of what's going on. Instead, it tells the world-wide evangelistic story in an impressionistic manner, and challenges Christians to join us in this great adventure of making Christ known to the ends of the earth.

Richard Kew
Cyril Okorocha

The Feast of St. Thomas the Apostle
December 21, 1995

CHAPTER ONE
The Life Blood of the Church

"Evangelism is not incidental to the life of the Church, it is fundamental to it. A church which does not engage in God's work of reconciliation is simply a disobedient church."
— THE MOST REV. GEORGE L. CAREY, SEPTEMBER 1995

The Rich Tapestry of Evangelism

A beautiful tapestry is a marvel. It is the product of months, perhaps years, of painstaking needlework, threads and colors being interwoven until the story has been told in pictures. Be it the dramatic Bayeux Tapestry's portrayal of the Battle of Hastings in 1066, or a magnificent *Akwete* crafted by the women of Imo River District in eastern Nigeria which hangs in a home to tell a human story or in a church illustrating some facet of the Christian faith, it is "a thing of beauty and a joy forever."

Evangelism has the same texture, warp and woof. Threads, colors, styles, and approaches are all interwoven and given shape and meaning under the sovereignty of God. The mission of the church is like such a tapestry, each color and thread being essential to the total glory and beauty of the whole. Maybe this was the greatest lesson of the conference held in Kanuga, North Carolina, in September 1995, which went by the unwieldy name of the Global Conference for Dynamic Evangelism beyond the year 2000 — or G-CODE 2000, for short.

Perhaps there are as many approaches to sharing faith as there are people who do it; what we have outlined in the following pages is a mere cross-section. Each intersects with the other, and it might be an accumulation of different approaches which ultimately leads a person to Christ, or which are used effectively in a parish somewhere.[1] Christians are called to be faithful in the work of evangelism. God is the one who weaves the tapestry, taking our words and actions and giving them the power of the Spirit as they impact upon the lives of others. Our responsibility is to be sensitive to the prompting and leading of the Holy Spirit, and to be faithful to the one who called us, for it is God "who gives the increase."

Ruth Falls In Love

Ruth was a senior nurse at a military hospital in war-torn Biafra, the region which attempted to secede from Nigeria in the 1960s. In her native Igbo tongue, Ruth's name was Nma-Aku, which roughly translates "Money Cannot Buy Beauty," or "Beauty Is Wealth." During that awful crisis which was then tearing his country apart, Cyril Okorocha, a teenager at the time, was working as an emergency medical assistant in the same hospital as Ruth.

One morning, the doctor away at the front, Cyril was going around the wards tending the patients. Suddenly, Ruth swooped down on him, with a young army lieutenant in tow. Her face sparkled, and there was an uncontrollable joy and excitement about her Cyril had never seen before.

"What's happening?" Cyril asked curiously, "Have you come into a lot of money, or something?"

She shook her head, displaying the whiteness of her teeth as she smiled, "Something much better than that, and I couldn't keep it from you even if I tried." Her radiant smile was seraphic. She burst out, "I'm in love!" She turned, and almost like a general, ordered the young officer, Paul Okelu, to step forward and be introduced.

Introductions over, Ruth hardly missed a beat as she bubbled, "Isn't he charming? It's impossible for me to keep this from you — or anyone else in the world, for that matter."

A quarter century has passed, but Ruth's falling in love is still fresh in Cyril's memory. From hereon her whole life would be incomplete without him, and his name would always be on her lips. And that is how it should be. Telling others about the people we love is one of the most natural and human instincts of all.

If spreading the news of our own good fortune, be it discovering our life's partner, passing exams, buying a new car, or taking pride in the achievements of our children, is so normal, shouldn't telling the whole world about Jesus Christ be the normal heart of Christian discipleship? Why aren't we so overwhelmed by the implications of our encounter with him, that we do not experience utter frustration if we do not share the experience? Most of us have learned that sharing what is precious does not detract but enriches our satisfaction. We want to suggest that keeping the greatest news to ourselves could be the first step down a road which will eventually smother the vibrancy of our faith.

Gossiping the Gospel

At the outset of the Christian story, following the death of the martyr Stephen, a rage of persecution broke out against believers in Jerusalem, many of whom rightly fearing for their lives escaped from the city, fleeing beyond the reach of the angry authorities.[2] What is remarkable is that instead of wallowing in self-pity or bitterly railing against their oppressors as so many displaced persons are prone to do, we find them chattering away about their love for Christ.

It was ordinary men and women, transformed by God's power, who set about "gossiping the Gospel" to the whole world. From Jerusalem they made for the powerful and pagan Roman city of Antioch in Syria. Antioch was where the faith jumped its first major cultural barrier. There Gentiles were not only attracted by the Cross, but responded in surprising numbers to Christ's resurrection when they heard the story told by those refugee-missionaries. Our forebears in the faith were nicknamed "Christ-ians" in Antioch because they couldn't stop talking about Jesus Christ! He was their new love. What was it that Ruth said about her young man, "It's impossible to keep this from you — or from anyone else in the world for that matter"?

Something similar is happening today in innumerable parts of the world. In war-ravaged regions of southern Sudan, literally tens of thousands are turning over their lives to Christ and being baptized. Risking his personal safety, the Archbishop of Canterbury visited that region in 1994 and was deeply moved by what he saw. People who had known nothing but war and privation for more than 40 years were overflowing with the joy in Christ which life's hardships had heightened, rather than obscured.

From China to Chile, and even in parts of the older churches in the West, after centuries spent struggling with the cumulative and corrosive effects of secularity, there is exciting evidence that the Holy Spirit is moving in remarkable ways. In addition, there is the growing awareness among Christians of the importance of telling the story to the quarter of the world's burgeoning population who have still to hear the first whisper of the Good News. Christians are also realizing that there are hundreds of millions more who have had only minimal opportunities to respond. As our story unfolds it will become increasingly apparent that while much progress has been made, much still remains to be done. "Uhuru!" is the African word for freedom or liberation — countless human beings have yet to experience Christ's liberating power.

As disturbing as this is, and as huge as the challenge remains, today there are more Christians from more backgrounds, nationalities, languages, and ethnic groups then ever before. The overriding passion for millions is spreading the Good News. History has never seen such a huge cadre of missionaries, lay and ordained, working tirelessly and creatively to evangelize this planet. Many denominational families have declared this last decade of the second millennium a "Decade of Evangelism." Roman Catholics have gone so far as to challenge the churches to give Jesus a 2000th birthday present of a billion new believers. In many places the fervor for evangelism has never been higher.

The following pages are a "snapshot" of what is going on. This book might be described as a case study in evangelism and mission, the Anglican Communion being the lens through which we can focus upon the Gospel's spread around the world.[3] While details will differ from church to church, the Anglican story has much in common with all others. In some places half-heartedness has turned evangelism into a forgotten art, marginalized and for the most part pursued by a minority of enthusiasts. Wherever this is so, the health — even the survival — of the church is in jeopardy.

Elsewhere, making Christ known by word and deed is at the cutting edge of everything congregations do. Here parishes are growing — sometimes at a phenomenal rate and, if it were possible, the Decade of Evangelism to which Anglicans have committed themselves seems to have stimulated a quickening of the pace. A further encouragement is the growing willingness of some who have been falling down on the job to listen to and learn from those whose prayers and evangelistic efforts are being blessed. Increasingly, this means older churches sitting at the feet of those younger churches they once helped to plant.

A Generation from Extinction?

The Christian church is never more than a generation from extinction. While there is a degree of hype in this statement, it illustrates the fundamental truth re-stated by George Carey, Archbishop of Canterbury, that "evangelism is not incidental to the life of the Church."[4] Evangelism must be the church's governing principle. "One generation from extinction" warns Christian communities who fail to make Christ known while continuing to live on past capital, that they themselves will shortly be turned into a mission field for other religions if they are not careful. Today there are plenty of religious groups, ancient or surprisingly modern, eager to fill the vacuum Christians leave as they retreat from obedience to Christ's Great Commission to take the message into all the world.[5] The pages of history are replete with warnings.

The Diocese of Wakefield, like everywhere else in England, is full of historic churches. Many of its 250 parishes are ancient foundations with centuries of Christian witness under their belts. However, when the present bishop, Nigel McCulloch, arrived in 1992 he was horrified by the statistics. No matter how they massaged them, it was impossible to put a good spin on the figures. The message was stark: if they refused to look reality in the face, by 2020 there would likely be no Anglicans left in that corner of northern England.

But the challenge facing this particular diocese has an added twist. In the last fifty years the local ethnic mix has changed radically. Since World War II, tens of thousands of Asian immigrants have settled there, many with an enthusiastic commitment to Islam. Christians who live in the area known as the Diocese of Wakefield might have grown passive, but the children and grandchildren of those Muslim newcomers are not. Today right in the heart of the diocese is what is probably the largest center for training Islamic evangelists in Europe. Those Muslim missionaries, far from regarding the materialistic world into which they go as a bleak, secular landscape, see this worldly paganism, born out of a rejection of Christianity, as a fertile harvest field.

This precipitous Christian decline had to be stopped. Bishop McCulloch and his team determined that when 2020 rolled around their diocese would still in business, and would be much more than a caretaker of historic buildings. The time had come to risk and to make changes. They even modified the name of the diocese to press the point home. Wakefield's Christians can be under no illusions about their plight, now finding themselves members of "The MISSIONARY Diocese of Wakefield." This is the first time in at least ten centuries that an English diocese has accepted such a designation, but it illustrates the determination with which this challenge is being faced in a place where the faith was once firmly entrenched. The Church of England might be the historic church of the land, but the course being steered in Wakefield demonstrates how much England has become a mission field to all comers.

This willingness to face the facts is having a dramatic outcome. First, Wakefield's Anglicans, led by their bishop, have unashamedly committed themselves to evangelism using all the resources at their disposal. Secondly, for the first time in years, the diocese is growing. It may only have seen a 1% expansion in 1994. But, as the saying goes, every journey begins with just one step. These initial signs of new growth are, so far, not tempting them to ease off and slide back into their old ways. The bishop continues to take every opportunity to call his people to evangelism. Again and again in the following pages, we will see that whenever bishops and other leaders champion evangelism — becoming *vision bearers* — the people follow and the whole church is mobilized.

The Broad Continuum of Mission and Evangelism

If you had visited an aging suburb of north London as the light faded one evening in early summer 1995, you might have seen a middle-aged woman walking slowly with her elderly mother from a gray stone church to their car. The older woman, bent and frail, had grown up in central Europe. She and her husband had fled from Nazi troops as they occupied their homeland. The Communist grab for power following World War II ended hopes the family had of returning home. A widow, old and ailing, she now lived with her daughter's family, suffering many of those worrying ailments that accompany extreme old age.

Usually, when her daughter needed to leave her mother for a few hours, she could find someone to sit with her. On this particular evening, her husband away on business, she struck out. Reluctantly, she decided to take her mother to the meeting she had to attend at her parish church. The reason for her misgivings was simple; since committing her own life to Christ as an adolescent, her mother had sometimes been quite hostile to her faith. As they settled in the car for the short ride home, the older woman, who had sat at the back of the meeting, turned to her daughter and said, "You talk a lot about conversion, don't you?" The daughter nodded, bracing herself for what might come next. Her mother's words were unexpected, wistful, even accusatory. "Then why haven't you tried to convert me in all these years?"

The daughter was stunned. She had sensed something hovering in the background all day but had not been able to put her finger on it. Now she realized it had been the Holy Spirit preparing them both for this moment. Taking a deep breath and shooting an unspoken prayer heavenward, she explained the Gospel, and had the joy of helping her mother over the threshold she had crossed so many years before.

At exactly the same time, less than twenty miles away, Anglican leaders from all over the world were gathered for serious business. "WorldReach" was a consultation convened by the Church Mission Society. Their task was to pray and think about the 21st century. They were concerned about reaching the unreached — those who as yet have had no chance to meet the risen Christ. Their minds were focused on the big picture, and how a strategy might be framed. The gathering began hatching bold strategies for Anglicans to play their part in the completion of world evangelization, marrying both skills and resources from churches in the global North as well as the global South. Much praying went on and many good ideas emerged. Some are bound to shape the way Anglicans — and perhaps other Christians — engage in mission for years to come.

These two very different incidents illustrate the breadth of the evangelistic task. At its heart are individuals and family groups meeting Jesus Christ as Lord and Savior, every personal encounter being a building block in a much bigger story. As God moves and people respond, Christians are being called to understand and formulate the part they should play in God's mission to present the message of the Kingdom to the whole world. Evangelism is a gigantic continuum, reaching outward in a sometimes bewildering kaleidoscope of strategies that include everything from the transformation of the lives of individuals close by, to enabling the same miracle to take place in a mountain village or burgeoning city on the other side of the world.

The Life Blood of the Church

The Gospel is about utter transformation — of individuals, cultures, and societies. The Body of Christ is God's human agent in this transforming work. As we teeter on the verge of a new millennium, with a variety of special evangelistic efforts in full swing, the time has come to review our progress, make course corrections, then move confidently forward, knowing God will provide both resources and opportunities. Many churches, especially those in the West, waste far too much time trying to define what their mission is, while expending too little effort sharing the message.

Evangelism is not a frill, some optional extra tagged onto the life of the church merely for the congenitally over-enthusiastic. Evangelism is our life blood. A church that walks away from evangelism, to all intents and purposes has ceased to be a church. Evangelism is not necessarily a comfortable business, and at times it can even be dangerous.   Yet, as anyone knows who has helped someone meet Christ, nothing is more exciting.

Raymond Fung, a religious journalist from Hong Kong, told Anglicans in conference in North Carolina in September 1995 that "Evangelism is the sharpest end of mission. It is the cutting edge of the church's encounter with the world." That is the message of our book!

◆◆◆◆◆

Holy Spirit of God,
all-powerful as the wind you came to the Church on the
Day of Pentecost to quicken its life and empower its witness.
Come to us now as the Wind of Heaven and breathe new life
into our souls; and revive your work among us, that God in all
things may be glorified, through Jesus Christ our Lord. Amen

A Prayer of the Church of England

What we have said:

■ From the Acts of the Apostles to the present moment, an eagerness to proclaim the Good News has been a characteristic of a healthy church.

■ Churches which refuse to witness effectively in word and deed are turned into mission fields for other religions in a few short decades.

■ For the first time in more than 1,000 years an English diocese has designated itself a MISSIONARY region, and such courageous honesty is having encouraging results.

■ Evangelism is a continuum stretching from individual conversions, to strategies to take the message of Christ to all people everywhere.

■ Evangelism is the cutting edge of the church's encounter with the world.

Thinking it over:

■ Read Acts 8.1-3, 11.19-30. Discuss what it might have been like to be in the shoes of those first disciples. Use your imagination to see how they would have involved themselves in evangelism, and what the passage might be saying to us today.

■ Is the notion that the church is a generation from extinction true, or is it a scare tactic?

■ How much of the continuum from personal witness to being involved in reaching into all the world is your congregation participating in? How can it get more involved?

■ Is evangelism the life blood of your church? If not, why, and what changes need to be made to make it so?

■ Wherever and whenever bishops and clergy become *Vision Bearers*, leaders wholeheartedly committed to God's mission, there is often renewal — even revival — and the church grows. Discuss this in light of Acts 6.2-7.

CHAPTER TWO
A Variety of Evangelisms

"Evangelism is a human attempt to waken or to reawaken personal faith in Jesus Christ." — RAYMOND FUNG

Christ's coming into the world was something like a stone being thrown into a pond, the ripple effect inexorably spreading outward from Jerusalem. Two thousand years later, the message of salvation has the power of dynamite for some, while for others it is little more than a vague echoing folk memory. Meanwhile, the news has yet to reach millions more. In some places the evangelistic task is to proclaim the message for the very first time, while in others the job is to jolt people from their apathy, and encourage them to take another look at this Man who has the power to turn the world upside down. In this chapter we intend to look more closely at the evangelistic continuum, attempting to see the way in which the world is being evangelized or re-evangelized today.

Renewal for Evangelism

Chinedu Nebo is an energetic man with an infectious smile. In addition to being a priest of the Nigerian church, he is a metallurgic engineer, and a world authority in his field.[1] But his primary mission is sharing the Good News of Jesus Christ. A gifted evangelist, he has traveled the length and breadth of his country leading missions and training a new generation of evangelists. On weekends and in university vacations he will travel with teams of students for Christian witness, or to teach evangelism, prayer and Christian discipleship in dioceses, deaneries or parishes.

Many African countries where the church maintains its witness, he tells Western friends, are "kleptocracies."[2] Yet despite this backdrop of gnawing corruption, unbridled inflation, and abject poverty, the church "continues to move ahead, and the gates of hell cannot prevail against it.'" Stories of the triumphs of the Christian Gospel in Africa roll readily from his tongue as he tells of exciting evangelistic missions.   Each story illustrates the integrity of his claim, demonstrating the renewing power of God. His experience corroborates the assertion we have already made, that a church which prays and evangelizes is bound to be a healthy church.

One of the best illustrations of this fact is the manner in which the Nigerian Church launched the Decade of Evangelism. In April 1991 at a vast celebration, the Archbishop of Nigeria consecrated nine bishops, and on behalf of the church charged eight of them to plant missionary dioceses in parts of northern Nigeria where Islam is both strong and aggressive. When they began, these dioceses were a mere handful of tiny, struggling congregations, and in some there was little or no Christian presence of any kind. Four years later things have started to change. In Sokoto, for example, there are already eleven thriving parishes, and even as we write they are following through on their commitment to grow to at least twenty parishes, each with a membership of more than 200 by the end of the century. Dr. Nebo is right; the Holy Spirit is moving, and God is building the church in Africa — sometimes against all odds.

But things have not always been this way in Nigeria. A generation ago, the church in this huge West African country of more than 120 million inhabitants was lethargic, and exhibited many of the less desirable characteristics afflicting European or North American Christianity. The Anglican Church in Nigeria could easily have taken the downward path trodden by these Western churches.

In the mid-1960s, Biafra, formerly the eastern region of Nigeria, declared its independence. Extraordinarily, in the midst of the bloody turmoil that ensued, God sowed seeds of spiritual renewal. The young men and women who experienced Christ during that tragic time are today the lay leaders, bishops, scholars, and evangelists of a revivified Nigerian church. Fires kindled in hearts then, continue to burn now and are spreading. Today the Church in Nigeria, with more than 11 million members, is the largest province of the worldwide Anglican Communion. It continues to grow at an astonishing pace, especially among the young, and is reaching into parts of the country hardly touched by the Gospel.

Stories of God moving in power in the church are not limited to Africa. From all over the Two-Thirds World comes news of astounding growth, often despite persecution, harassment, and legal restraint. In early 1995, the late Bishop of West Malaysia reported that in the previous five years his diocese had grown from 50 parishes and mission stations to more than 150. What is most significant is that much of this advance has taken place since the bishop experienced healing and an extraordinary in-filling of the Holy Spirit in 1992. This fresh encounter with the risen Christ turned him into a *Vision Bearer*, and set his diocese alight!

Primary Evangelism

While in much of the West the church is in the doldrums, sometimes struggling just to keep its head above water, in Africa and parts of Asia and Latin America the cause of Christ surges ahead. Congregations are multiplying with such rapidity that dioceses are forced to divide, then sub-divide again, in an effort to keep up with the pastoral challenge of burgeoning numbers. This amazing growth stems from a commitment to primary evangelism — the task of taking the Good News to individuals at the grass roots.[3]

Take the Anglican Evangelistic Association, for example. The Association was established in 1988 in Tanzania following the call from all the Anglican bishops that the last decade of this millennium should be a "Decade of Evangelism." The brainchild of a group of clergy and laity, its goal is to take the message of Christ to all the world, and to "rekindle (the) living faith in the Churches in the Anglican Communion."[4] The Association now supports seven evangelistic teams, whose ministry is coordinated by David Haji. David is a slight, soft-spoken man, whose family was converted from Islam not long before he was born.

David Haji sensed God calling him to the work of evangelism about the time he graduated from business college. Today he manages the Association's affairs, coordinates the mission teams, and leads one himself. His face comes alive when he describes how they identify, then pray for areas targeted for evangelism. These are normally places, urban or rural, where there is little Christian witness. Missions take a variety of forms depending on the nature of the community, and might include everything from house-to-house visitation, to open-air preaching in towns and villages. Constant intercessory prayer is fundamental to their strategy.

Often the witness is backed up by movies. They have discovered that a projector and generator, taken into an area where there is no electricity, can draw huge crowds. Each evening they will show Christian movies, especially "The Jesus Film," a production which has been seen by literally hundreds of millions all over the world since the early 1980s.[5] The movies are followed up by preaching, and this often elicits a considerable response.

Even amidst the all too frequent bloody turmoil which has afflicted Africa in the last few generations, Christians have not shirked their responsibility to make Christ known. The horrifying acts of genocide and tribal massacre in the heavily evangelized nation of Rwanda, unleashed by a complex mixture of forces, has profound and disturbing implications for the churches, yet even in the seeming hopelessness of refugee camps in Tanzania and Zaire, amazing numbers have been turning to Christ anew. For example, on one Sunday in August 1995, Bishop Edwin Nyamubi of Kagera, Tanzania, confirmed 754 Rwandan refugees in a camp at Rumasi. The previous week he had confirmed 687 in another camp, and on the following Sunday would be presented with 714 candidates. Similar stories abound in Sudanese camps. One of the great challenges facing these churches is how to teach the people the fundamentals of the faith — and the ethical implications of Christian belief.

At the Global Conference for Dynamic Evangelism (G-CODE 2000) in North Carolina in September 1995, Diana Witts, General Secretary of England's Church Mission Society, told of a recent visit to southern Sudan. In the midst of a war almost forgotten by the rest of the world, explosive growth is taking place. There are mass conversions among tribes like the Dinkas, a group who had previously seemed all but impervious to Christianity. Now the Spirit is moving in the midst of the poverty and utter dehumanization caused by this seemingly endless conflict, and huge numbers are pouring into the churches. Where there was only a handful of struggling congregations not long ago, scores of new congregations are being planted, while the "older" churches are crammed with hundreds of members. "In human terms there is no reason for anything but despair," she said, and yet, with material securities swept aside and dependent for everything on God alone, the faith is surging ahead. The growth of this unique church is astonishing — and for the moment at least, seems unstoppable.

Western Christians, living in secular wastelands, look on with a mixture of awe and envy at this extraordinary growth in Africa, but this spread of the faith is not accidental. These churches pray earnestly, and have made evangelism their top priority. Consequently, they are able to establish ambitious targets, and then will work tenaciously toward them, all the time prayerfully seeking God's blessing and guidance. One of the notable mid-century Bishops of Central Tanganyika was the late Alfred Stanway, an Australian. Bishop Stanway would constantly remind his people that, "If you aim at nothing, you're bound to hit it!" Western churches have forgotten this lesson, meanwhile the Africans have learned it well.

While many Western churches flounder without much sense of direction, the Africans, guided by the Holy Spirit and working fields ripe for harvest, have sought to make Christ known in every corner of their continent — sometimes in spite of odds heavily stacked against them. It is foolish to romanticize the African church; they themselves are the first to admit their many shortcomings, yet God is honoring their commitment to reach out with the Gospel of salvation.

To Re-Evangelize the West

In fun-loving, secularized Australia, Christians face a hard uphill struggle. Spiritual moorings which once anchored the nation have been cut, and the churches now face the daunting task of re-evangelizing a cynical population. The Anglican Church in Australia is wrestling with statistics which in certain states even make those from Wakefield look encouraging. Anglicans nominally comprise 23% of the population of 17 million, yet on any given Sunday there will be less than 100,000 people in Australia's Anglican parishes.

A similar slide has been experienced across the Tasman Sea in New Zealand. New Zealand, now often called Aotearoa out of respect for its Maori population, is a country which some

Christians think could fairly lay claim to the title of being the world's most secularized land. Only two dioceses have experienced any growth during the 1990s; seven others watch numbers dwindle. What makes matters worse is the observation by some that segments of their church seem skeptical about the value of evangelism at all. One New Zealand priest suggested that their church is "a highly dysfunctional family needing divine intervention if we are to get it right."

Bleak stories like these from Australia and New Zealand can be replicated all over the Western world. Indeed, throughout the West churches seem overwhelmed by cultures which "are secular, humanistic, individualistic, pluralistic, fragmented, materialistic, consumer-oriented, pragmatic and sensate,"[6] and it is proving extraordinarily demanding to re-present Christ to a culture that has rejected or tried to forget him. Across the Pacific you might find proportionately more Canadians in church on any given Sunday than Australia or New Zealand, but the Anglican Church there is wrestling with statistics every bit as discouraging. Behind the numbers lie countless distressing stories of accelerating decline. Extinction could also be in the cards for the Canadian church within a generation if priorities are not changed.

At first glance things do not seem quite so grim in the USA, where small gains in numbers were recorded in the mid-1990s, but scratch beneath the surface and the same theme emerges. In certain parts of the country decline is catastrophic, dioceses losing as many as 50% of members in a quarter century — and the slide continuing unabated. The Episcopal Church has shed one third of its membership since the mid-1960s, despite the rapid growth of the American population, and wrestles with bitter internal divisions. Numbers might not tell the whole story, but it is puzzling that so relatively few Episcopalians are worried by such depressing statistics.

The churches in the New World and Pacific are not alone. The scene is the same in Europe and the British Isles. But the picture is not universally grim. There are pockets of great encouragement, with parishes and dioceses catching the vision, because they have dedicated themselves to the apostolic faith and evangelism. As more churches learn from the experience of those who are making such progress, these pockets of health can be expanded, and might eventually turn into a mighty groundswell.

Wellington and Nelson are the two dioceses in New Zealand which have grown during the last five years. There is obviously something exhilarating happening in Nelson where attendances have shot up by more than 30% since 1990, and one careful observer has suggested it might be the fastest growing diocese in the Western world. There are growing numbers of towns and cities in the West, where you will come across visionary Anglican churches that are bursting at the seams, exercising a rich array of ministries. Holy Trinity, Brompton, in London, as it sought to reach the skeptical and unchurched in a way that was warm and unthreatening, developed an enjoyable series which they have dubbed "The Alpha Course." Alpha principles have been thoroughly tried and tested, and are proving so effective that the course is now being used all over Britain and is spreading to other parts of the "developed" world.[7]

One American bishop told us that a majority of the parishes in his diocese are bursting out of their buildings, and in the last decade an unprecedented number of new congregations have been established there — and this after 30 years of constant decline. Elsewhere in the USA, a diocese which has seen little growth for years has recorded a 16% increase in membership in a 24 month period. These days, almost everywhere Anglicans realize there is much to be learned from those who are making progress in the midst of secularity, whether they be Baptists, Pentecostals, or new denominations like the Vineyard Fellowship of Churches.[8]

On returning from a recent visit to Latin America, Professor David Martin told English Christians that the traditional mainline churches there did not seem able to touch the religious ethos of the people. "There is a constant breakaway from these churches and consequent establishment of new (often pentecostal and evangelical) ones under young, Bible-believing local leadership."[9] He went on to indicate that in the last generation the Roman Catholic Church could well have lost as much as 10% of its membership in this way. Such splintering off is not only confined to the Latin world. Most evangelical and pentecostal churches in Africa and parts of Asia today are led by local young visionaries. They have often splintered from mainline denominations which have either failed to recognize or refused to open themselves to the movement of God's renewing and reviving Spirit.

Churches in the post-Christendom West are clearly facing

enormous difficulties which leave many feeling discouraged. Thankfully, others are realizing that the seismic changes now reshaping the world's social, political, and religious landscape offer an array of possibilities — a veritable new beginning. Princeton's Diogenes Allen thinks the West is passing through a period of cultural lag, however "when the dust settles," we will realize "the fields are ripe for the harvest."[10]   Western culture, once rooted and grounded in the faith, now cries out for re-evangelization, he intimates. Christians are increasingly willing to admit that their spiritual strength has been sapped, and that instead of witnessing into their secular environment they have often allowed themselves to be coopted by it. Today they struggle to grasp what it means to be a healthy counter-culture in a world which is spiritually ravenous.

It is not beyond the bounds of possibility that the churches in the West could actually be poised to become an exciting alternative to the tired emptiness of self-indulgence, hedonism, and unbridled materialism. Yet re-evangelization is no easy task, demanding radical, and sometimes very uncomfortable changes in the churches, if they are to grasp this opportunity. On returning to Britain after a lifetime of mission service, Lesslie Newbigin remarked that the churches in the West are situated on "the most difficult missionary frontier in the contemporary world."[11]

The enthusiastic and growing churches in the global South have an important role to play in this recovery of lost ground in what was once the heartland of Christianity — that is, if their "Northern" sisters and brothers will allow them. Leaders in the South have started offering their gifts and resources for "the re-evangelization of the North," and for dynamic partnership in truly global mission.   An exciting development in the Anglican Communion is not just the eagerness with which newer churches are taking up this challenge, but the willingness with which some older churches are accepting the help proffered. CMS in England and Ireland have taken up this offer, while the Chilean church has effectively deployed missionaries in Spain — at the request of the Reformed Episcopal Church there.[12]

Evangelizing the Unevangelized

From the Atlantic coast of North Africa, across the Middle East, through Central Asia, and all the way to the furthest end of the

Indonesian archipelago, lies a swathe of the planet where the Christian faith is making little impact — or has lost its grasp of ground once held. Except for pockets like Kerala in South India, Christians are no more than a tiny proportion of the population, and in some ethnic groups and megacities there are few, if any, believers at all. This region is a patchwork of political, religious, and ethnic colors, many of which either disdain or are hostile to Jesus Christ.

This chunk of the planet has been dubbed "World A" by mission strategists, who believe it deserves the highest priority for prayer, mission and evangelism. Some 2 to 3 billion people, perhaps 40% of the world's population are to be found in this zone, a vast majority of whom have never even heard the Christian message. What makes "World A" so challenging is that it contains what one missiologist calls, "some of the most formidable traditional barriers to the gospel."[13]

Considerable numbers of Christians living and witnessing in "World A" live out their faith in an environment of constant harrassment and persecution. They might be treated as second-class citizens in their own lands, and often it is illegal for them even to mention the name of Jesus Christ to outsiders. In many of the ethnic groups in this zone there are few, if any, Christians at all, while it might be illegal for foreign missionaries from either East or West to enter the country, live there, and attempt to establish a church. Those with a burden for these least evangelized peoples are experimenting with a variety of approaches which break with previous missionary models once and for all.

One of the foremost champions of "World A" is Anglican priest, researcher, and "retired" CMS missionary, David B. Barrett. Dr. Barrett has been summoning Christians to take seriously the challenge of these "unreached people groups" for many years. He estimates that of the 13,000 distinct ethnicities on earth, at least 4,000 remain totally unevangelized — and a vast majority are to be found in "World A". In mid-1995 he argued that "the next five years clearly represent a strategic opportunity for the proper deployment of missionaries."[14]

The potential harvest of new Christians is huge, but relatively few are striving to bring them the message of Christ. One of Barrett's most shocking estimates is that more church money is actually embezzled by Christian leaders each year, than all the churches everywhere invest in making Christ known among the least evangelized of "World A". While hundreds of thousands of evangelists and missionaries are working in places already heavily evangelized, a mere handful funded by less than 1% of the world's missionary budgets are working among these "unreached peoples."[15]

Anglicans have been pioneers in reaching the unreached during the last two centuries. A thriving Communion of some 70 million members is the fruit of these efforts. Yet today Anglicans often seem so caught up in the complexities of being a worldwide Communion, that they are in danger of losing sight of those least evangelized peoples. Thankfully, some are realizing our omission. Dioceses in Southeast Asia are starting to reach out to unreached peoples, while CMS's WorldReach consultation, alluded to earlier, is evidence that the unreached and under-evangelized are fast rising on the church's agenda. In 1992, the Anglican Frontier Missions was established in Richmond, Virginia. AFM is pioneering the use of modern communications possibilities to reach beyond the frontiers, and the use of modern data-gathering and analysis to enable the task.[16]

Encouraging as all this might be, the time is long overdue for burgeoning Anglican churches in the global South and the relatively resource-rich churches in the global North to explore and experiment with new ways of working together to commit resources and personnel to this great unfinished task. Should we discover how to make this happen, then look out for the profound impact this would have upon churches at home! History shows us that when mission is a priority, it has a way of generating renewal among the churches who get involved.

Seeds Have Been Planted

Even in those places where the Gospel is not being proclaimed, God is seldom without some kind of witness. Reports of increasing numbers of life-changing encounters with Christ are filtering out of the predominantly Islamic world, where there are unknown numbers of "secret believers." In one place there might be a clandestine Bible study, while somewhere else a young woman — or even a *mullah* — meets the Lord Jesus in a vision or dream. Perhaps God's most astounding strategy today, is to reach into the

Islamic word using dreams and visions. There is a steady increase in reports of visions of Christ, even the Virgin Mary, in Muslim settings — even one recently reported in a mosque in West Africa.

In relatively few places with a large Islamic majority can Christians function openly. Yet where this is possible, their love and willingness to reach out to the poor and downtrodden have gained them the respect — sometimes grudging — of Muslim neighbors. They are prepared to go out of their way to aid refugees or provide medical care to those who otherwise could not afford a doctor. There are tales galore we would love to shout from the housetops, but hostility in some Islamic countries is so intense, we refrain from doing so to protect our fellow-believers. We urge that prayers be made for Christians laboring in these difficult places. One Arab Christian has said, "Living in a Muslim country is like finding the way when there are other proclamations and challenges being presented." Those who live out their faith in such places bring new meaning to our Lord's injunction to be the light shining in a dark place.[17]

While Islam stretches from the Atlantic to eastern Indonesia, as we travel further East other great religions — and enigmatic spiritualities — come into play. Churches in southeast Asia proclaim Christ in societies bound by the web of Buddhism, while Indian churches work against an increasingly militant Hindu backdrop. Yet even where hostile religious pressures make life difficult for believers, God is redeeming people.

The evidence suggests that if the churches pay closer attention to and allocate resources for mission there, amazing numbers would find their way into the fold. Studies are beginning to suggest that if the same amount of time, treasure, talent, energy and prayer were focused on making Christ known in these overlooked places, as is committed to already heavily evangelized areas, the slow spread of the flame of faith could be turned into a raging forest fire![18]

But fascinating things are happening. The Anglican Church in Lautoka, Fiji, has grown by 25% in the four years leading up to 1995. More than half the new converts come from a Hindu background, while the city-nation of Singapore, a mish-mash of ethnicities and religions, is home of one of the most exciting dioceses in the Anglican world. Although the bulk of its parishes are on the tiny island of Singapore proper, the huge geographical area which makes up the rest of the diocese stretches through six countries, with a combined population of 300 million people. This probably makes it the most populous single Anglican diocese in the world. Not only has there been very little Christian witness in many of these lands, but apart from English-speaking chaplaincies, Anglicans have hardly ventured into them — until now.

Led by a visionary bishop, Singapore has designated these nations as deaneries, each of which is then linked with a group of parishes at home, who are encouraged to involve themselves in outreach there. Their strategy is showing signs of working as they reach into Cambodia, Vietnam, Thailand, Laos and Indonesia — where they are working with an unreached people group. New congregations are being planted. They have also trained and sponsored nationals from these various countries who have been converted to Christ while living in Singapore, often as economic refugees, and then supported them as they have gone back to their homelands with the Gospel.

Evangelistic and medical teams from Singapore regularly travel to these places. These visits fuel their prayer, and far from detracting from the ministry at home, encourage congregations to more wholeheartedly witness locally. Most Singaporean parishes are networks of cell groups, many of which pray for and support work being done. As the stories of God at work in the deaneries come back, the enthusiasm of the parishioners is further heightened. Singapore is a fascinating model that dioceses elsewhere might consider emulating as we face up to the challenge of "World A".

Wise Words from the East

Bishop Datuk Yong Ping Chung is a bespectacled, scholarly Chinese with a passion for evangelism. His is an infectious, soft-spoken holiness, with the aura of a "wise Christian mandarin." One of the acknowledged leaders of evangelism and mission in the Anglican Communion, Yong Ping Chung is bishop of the Diocese of Sabah on the island of Borneo. It is illegal for Christians in this part of Malaysia to present Christ to the Muslims, who comprise 55% of the population.

When the world's Anglicans met in the mountains of North Carolina in September 1995 to focus on evangelism, Bishop Ping Chung preached the opening sermon. He playfully pointed out that we are often so eager to do churchy things, that we forget about Christ, essentially leaving him behind. With twinkling eyes he retold the story of Jesus meeting the Samaritan woman at the well in Sychar.[19] This happened, he joked, while the disciples were off in town doing "church work," — looking for food for their group — "Chinese take away." He compared them to vestries or parish councils which so often get side-tracked doing things that are "really important," so that they miss out on evangelistic openings.

The opportunities are always there to introduce people to Christ, he told his audience, but "when (an opportunity) is gone, it is gone forever." He shook his head sadly over our blindness to the chances God gives us. "In our busy schedule, in our busy parish activities, in our busy dioceses, it is easy to miss the point. Our eyes, our faith and our local church are built on a security which is totally immaterial to Jesus at this point. The call by Lambeth 88[20] is the call to move out of the safe waters of maintenance into the sea of primary evangelism, to get a new vision and new priority so that we can meet the spiritual needs of millions of people who do not know Jesus Christ."[21] The bishop's words were echoed and re-echoed for a whole week. Almost everyone left realizing anew the urgency of the task.

O Lord God,
You have called your Church to witness for you in this world.
Help us to publish the good news, not only in word so that
everyone can understand, but also by our deeds of love. Give us
the strength and courage always to stand up for righteousness,
justice and peace and may what we do now and throughout the
Decade of Evangelism be a blessing to all, especially the poor, the
powerless, the oppressed, the sick and indeed all those around us
who do not know Christ as Savior, Liberator, Healer and the Giver
of the abundant life of joy, forgiveness, holiness, and fulfillment.
We ask this in His Name. Amen

(A slight adaptation of a prayer from the Church in the West Indies)

What we have said:

■ God renews the church, not so it can enjoy itself with spiritual self-indulgence, but for the task of evangelism and mission.

■ African churches are often so successful in evangelism because they make it a priority, nurture a vision, work with a strategy, and soak their ministry in intercessory prayer.

■ Secularity is corrosive, eating away at the vitals of churches. Nevertheless, people are spiritually hungry. Vast tracts of the planet need re-evangelizing.

■ There are more than one billion people in "World A" who are completely unreached. Taking the Gospel to them must be a priority

■ God does not leave even the least hospitable places in the world without a witness. Current experience in many "closed" places corroborates this.

■ When an evangelistic opportunity is lost, it may be lost forever.

Thinking it over:

■ Do you think the fruits of spiritual renewal have been used as a springboard for mission, or have they been squandered on self-indulgence? If you think the latter, why, and what would be a positive way forward?

■ Why do you think intercessory prayer is so important for effective evangelism?

■ What are the benefits of having a measurable evangelistic strategy?

■ Has your congregation any vision for reaching those in "World A"? If not, what do you think you can do to rectify this situation?

■ Read John 4.1-38. What does it tell us about urgency in Jesus's ministry and world evangelization, including the re-evangelization of today's secular world?

CHAPTER THREE
In Cooperation with Other Christians

"The church was born internationally and ecumenically right from the beginning in Jerusalem."
— THE RT. REV. SAMIR KAFITY, BISHOP OF JERUSALEM

It is God's Mission

"When the left hand consents to a willing right hand, and the right hand washes the left hand in turn, then both hands will become clean," is one of the wise sayings of the Igbo people of southeastern Nigeria. They are convinced that their strength as a people, even their survival, is bound up with their unity. When someone, especially a wealthy person, is arrogantly self-reliant they tell them, "no one buries themselves effectively; if they attempted to do so one of their hands would have to be left outside — to nail down the lid of the coffin and to shovel earth into the grave!"

On the night before he died, our Lord prayed that his church would be united.[1] He recognized that each Christian or group of Christians was dependent upon others if there was going to be an effective witness to the Gospel.[2] Jesus' words have been echoed by Christian leaders down through the centuries, not least the present Archbishop of Canterbury: "Unity is fundamental to the mission of the church in the world."[3]

One of the many temptations to disunity is the belief by too many Christians that all mission initiatives are theirs and theirs alone, when in reality mission belongs to God. The Latin tag,

Missio Dei[4] has been applied to the church's work for generations, and it presses this point home. God calls us to partnership in this divine task — alongside believers of all linguistic, ethnic, and denominational families. We are emissaries of the Almighty. As proud and comfortable as we might be with our denominational heritage, we should avoid arrogantly thinking we are able as Anglicans to go it alone. We all need each other in the Body of Christ.

The evangelistic challenge facing the worldwide Christian family today is so immense that it *must* be shared: South and North, voluntary and synodical agencies, church and parachurch organizations working together. Unless we cooperate, any dream of giving all persons everywhere a fair chance of hearing and responding to the Gospel message will remain no more than that. The worldwide Anglican Communion is one of the larger bodies of Christian believers with 70 million members. However, we are minuscule beside the planet's burgeoning population which will have reached more than six billion by 2001. Furthermore, a huge proportion of the world's people live geographically, linguistically, ethnically or politically beyond the reach of one of our churches. When we see the size of the challenge in these terms, even Roman Catholicism, the largest of all communions, appears very small indeed.

Let us re-state our point: the church exists for mission. Mission is our very reason for existing. God has called all churches and their parachurch colleagues — whether Catholic or Orthodox, Coptic or Anglican, Evangelical or Pentecostal, to share the *Missio Dei*, and to become a visible expression of it in today's world. This was in the mind of the Lambeth Conference of Bishops, when in 1988 they called for a Decade of Evangelism to round off the old millennium. The Decade is not meant to be a mere temporary change of agenda before we return once more to the business-as-usual mentality. The Decade of Evangelism signals a determination to make a permanent change. The bishops invited dioceses around the world to participate in this focused effort "in cooperation with other Christians."[5] The reason for this ecumenical overture is plain: not only was this obedience to Christ's vision, but while Anglicans were hatching their plans to reach out, other Christians, both in denominational families and interdenominational coalitions, were doing exactly the same thing.

In all, 23 decades of evangelism have been set in motion. Isn't it extraordinary that this vision has grasped the imaginations of so many churches at the same time? It is almost as though our minds are being directed back to the Day of Pentecost again. Could it be that God is calling all the churches to join forces in a whole-hearted commitment to bring in the final harvest. What a fascinating prospect this is for us to meditate and act upon.

Yet as we reach the mid-point of this final decade of the final century of the second millennium, it is sad how small the impact the various mission strategies to reach the world are making — and how little they intersect with each other. Given the close relationship between mission and unity in Christ's teaching, and the history of world evangelization, it would have been wonderful if Christians could have got beyond merely sharing minutes with one another by now. If airlines, computer manufacturers, and telecommunications giants are able to sink their differences in the global pursuit of profits, why do Christians find it so difficult to join forces in this most noble of all enterprises?

In many parts of the world, denominations have little relevance — either because Christians are such a tiny minority, or they have been superseded because of external pressures. In certain areas what were once competing missionary denominations have joined forces to become united churches, while in China denominations were outlawed by the Communist authorities in the 1950s. Yet some churches, especially those from the West, are guilty of exporting their divisions. Fragmentation, it is scornfully pointed out, is a "Western luxury."[6]

A respected leader of the Church of South India, the oldest and most successful uniting churches, grieved over this with us. There was sadness in his voice as he told of independent charismatic or evangelical groups, mostly from North America, setting up shop in parts of his country, often sapping the strength of existing CSI congregations in their witness to a predominantly Hindu population. Meanwhile, there are still several hundred thousand villages in India where there is no Christian witness at all.

But There are Some Bright Spots

In the predominantly Buddhist country of Myanmar (Burma), where life is not easy for minority religions, four denominations work together as much as possible. A Buddhism resurgence is being encouraged by the national government, often at the expense of other faiths. Having seen how Christians share their message, the Buddhists have established schools to train a cadre of enthusiastic young missioners.

But Buddhism isn't the churches' only spiritual challenge in this beautiful land. Superstition, witchcraft, and an array of cultic practices thrive, sometimes even reaching tentacles deep into all religious groups in the country — including the Christian church. As an aside: this evidence of syncretism shows that while evangelism is the proclamation of the Gospel by Christians working in fellowship with one another, "purifying" the church is of necessity a long, sometimes slow, didactic process, as Christ is formed in people's lives and values. Only when the faith is deeply rooted in the Lord and the Scriptures will the experience of conversion be both transforming and long-lasting.[7]

Furthermore, Islam, which has about the same number of adherents as the Christian faith in Myanmar, is also making a concerted effort to win the Burmese people. As elsewhere in the world, large sums of oil money are pouring in and are being invested in mosques, schools, and facilities like homes for the aged. Nominal Muslims are being reclaimed and Islamic missionary teams have developed their own strategy to win Burma to the Prophet.

Burmese Christians are a mere 6% of the population, so it is vital they stick together rather than allowing strength to be sapped by unnecessary rivalry. There are approximately 1.2 million Baptists, 500,000 Roman Catholics, 100,000 members of the Assemblies of God, and 55,000 Anglicans in Burma today, in addition to other smaller Christian groups. In a less fraught setting this broad array of believers would be unlikely to cooperate. Yet God is blessing their shared witness. All these churches lack a depth of leadership, which means that when an opportunity presents itself which one denomination cannot take on, it shares the opening with the others. It is not unusual for Roman Catholics and Baptists to work side-by-side — even ceding work to one another to achieve a common objective.

Much evangelism being undertaken by Burmese Christians is among people groups[8] who have been beyond the reach of the Gospel. These include tribal peoples, who make up a significant proportion of the population. As Communism ebbed in

Southeast Asia it left an ideological vacuum in its wake. Groups like the Wa, once growers of opium and supporters of a Chinese brand of Marxism, are revising their views and now welcome Christian missionaries — and whole communities are being converted. In Burma evangelists need to be hardy. Anglican, Pentecostal, Catholic and Baptist emissaries for Christ must be prepared to travel on foot for days through dangerous country to take the message to those who have yet to hear it — and God is blessing their endeavors.

What Can the Rest of the World Learn About Cooperation?

Life might not be easy for Christians in Myanmar, but there is much that churches in the rest of the world can learn from them about cooperation, rather than squabbling over our own interests and distinctives. Roman Catholics may talk about giving Jesus a 2,000th birthday present of one billion new believers, while others have worthy objectives like reaching every home on earth for Christ. Much *has* been achieved, but careful analysis reveals that these efforts have done little to accelerate the numbers meeting Christ. Is it too cynical to ask whether much of our efforts to date have more to do with internal renewal and domestic housecleaning than with actually taking the Gospel to outsiders? Working together, we need a strategy which is determined to reach outward.

The second half of these various Decades of Evangelism could be a time when churches and parachurch organizations begin discovering how to sink their differences and coordinate strategies, radically improving the ability of Christians to make Christ known the world over. One of the verses of Scripture which shaped the lives of both of us, one growing up in Nigeria, the other in England, was Christ's words, "The harvest is plenteous, but the laborers are few."[9]

A process of what the Catholic thinker, George Wiegel, calls "unsecularlization" is taking place everywhere.[10] People are spiritually sensitive as never before. All over the world, as a new kind of global culture emerges, Christians are being offered the opportunity of lifetimes. The harvest is indeed enormous, the mission is God's. As we cooperate with the Lord in this work, is it beyond the bounds of possibility that we might not also learn how to work more effectively with one another?

◆◆◆◆◆

The Lord prayed that we might have unity and oneness of
purpose, a singular commitment to seeking God's glory, and
made it decisive to the conversion of the world and the
credibility of our profession as his disciples.

My prayer... is for these who will believe in me...
that all of them may be one.
Father just as you are in me and I am in you,
May they be brought to complete unity
To let the world know that you sent me. Amen
(Christ's Prayer for the Church, John 17 vvs. 20-23)

What we have said:

■ It is God's Mission, not ours. Its Latin name is *Missio Dei.*

■ God calls Christians of every flavor and background to worship
him and share in this mission.

■ Cooperation in evangelism between Christians of many traditions is minimal, except in countries like Myanmar.

■ There is a close relationship between mission and unity.

■ Our Lord prayed for the *oneness* which he says is proof to the
world of his presence among us, and the authenticity of the One
sent by God — Jesus the Messiah.

Thinking it over:

■ Talk about why you think Christians find it so difficult to cooperate with one another in the work of mission and evangelism.

■ Why do you think cooperation goes better where the Christian
church is a minority or is despised and perhaps openly persecuted?

■ Read carefully the whole of John chapter 17 and see if you can
work out what Jesus is saying about the relationship between mission and unity.

■ In what specific ways can you apply the message of the Lord's
prayer for unity in John 17 to your own situation?

Chapter Four
More Opportunities Than We Know What to Do With!

"Never has there been a greater need for a courageous and faithful forthtelling of the Gospel than now."
— THE MOST. REV. GEORGE L. CAREY
ARCHBISHOP OF CANTERBURY

The Hinge of History

The world is passing through a period of unprecedented change. This statement is already one of the most over-used truisms of our time — people might even be getting bored by it. Yet it will have to be repeated again and again in the years ahead because the shifting environment will demand great changes in the church. While the message of Jesus Christ is "the same, yesterday, today, and forever,"[1] the way in which we project the salvation story into the rapidly emerging world will have to alter. This challenge should heighten the urgency to make the message known.

Times of transition are never easy, and the "hinge of history"[2] over which we are passing is virtually unparalleled. In the next couple of generations much that is familiar will be swept away, forcing us to reorder the way we think and to rearrange our priorities. Unless Christians are assiduous in our attempts to understand and respond to what is going on, we could find themselves stumbling around like sightless people in a room where someone has moved the furniture.

It is a sad fact that much of the church has not even begun to struggle with the implications of this emerging era, perhaps because most of us are not yet ready to accept the ramifications. The period of accelerating transformation through which our world is passing compares to the Renaissance, the Reformation, and the Industrial Revolution all rolled into one. What is more, this is not happening just in one corner of the world from where it will spread outward, but everywhere — and because of instant communications — all at once. The intensity of this is heightened by the sensation of psychological and social inertia which seems to be an inevitable side-effect of the approach of the new millennium.

Despite the underlying uncertainties, we need not be afraid. God is lord of time, invention, and history. Even a cursory understanding of the Christian story demonstrates that, time and again, massive global chapter changes turn out to be extraordinary opportunities for the Gospel. The telecommunications revolution, which has done so much to reshape the world, opens for us a vision of once unimaginable opportunities. These days no country or door can be considered closed to the Gospel, as has been the case in the past. The challenge now facing believers is learning to ride this "wave" like a skilled surfer, rather than allowing ourselves to lose balance and be sucked in by the undertow.

We are a privileged generation. We are being offered the opportunity to shape the *Missio Dei* not merely for another generation, but perhaps for the next 500 years — if Christ does not return in the meantime.

The Great Spiritual Depression is Over

You don't have to hang around for long with people from all over the world who are committed to the work of evangelism, to be overwhelmed by the massive opportunities facing the church on the eve of the new millennium. From early morning to late at night, on strolls in the woods or over corn flakes at breakfast, evangelism and mission are the major topics of conversation. The sheer magnitude of all that is happening eventually overloads the brain! This was the never-to-be-forgotten experience of those of us present at the G-CODE 2000 gathering in North Carolina. In the new friendships made, ideas exchanged, and networks developed, the Holy Spirit was at work.

At lunch one day you might find yourself sitting next to a

bearded Chilean talking passionately about his outreach among professionals in Santiago; across the table sits a woman from Sierra Leone, a bishop from Mozambique, or someone from Scotland. At the next meal your companions could be a Palestinian, a Sri Lankan, or a young man with a burning zeal for Christ from the Pacific island nation of Tonga. In a score of languages and from the four points of the compass came the unmistakable message that "Now is the time!"

Spiritual Hunger

A hurricane-force wind of change is sweeping the world, and perhaps Christians need to become aware of the hidden hand of God in all this. Not long ago, Eugene Peterson, speaking of the situation in North America, wrote,

> "There is a ground-swell of recognition spreading through our culture that all life is at root spiritual; that everything we see is formed and sustained by what we cannot see. Those of us who grew up in the Great Spiritual Depression and who accustomed ourselves to an obscure life in the shadow of arrogant Rationalism and bullying Technology can hardly believe our eyes and ears. People all around us — neighbors and strangers, rich and poor, Communists and capitalists — want to know about God..."[3]

What Professor Peterson says as an American, is something which resonates with others from different parts of the globe.

In the West there is a growing awareness that life is more than what can be seen, heard, smelled or felt. After several centuries of being conditioned by the blinkered and spiritually corrosive mindset which relegated God to the footnotes and instead enthroned progress, reason, science, freedom and technology, we now find ourselves moving into a time when people are realizing there is another dimension has been elbowed to one side. This does not mean that where secularization has taken hold there is likely to be a mad dash back to the churches, but it does mean people are nowhere near as confident in the materialistic worldview as they used to be. Every kind of spirituality, healthy, perverse, or downright evil, is being explored.

But unlike yesteryear, Christians no longer have the field to themselves when it comes to the affairs of the soul. If we are to benefit from this extraordinary turn of events, we must learn to present Jesus Christ with meaning and passion within this animated marketplace of ideas. People are frantic to find some kind of credible belief system or worldview. This is precisely what the Christian faith is, and if meaningfully presented by those with an authentic lifestyle, seekers are bound to be brought face to face with the holy, living God.

An American, rector of a prestigious parish in the Old South, described a recent conversation with his youth leader about the way ministry among teenagers has altered since his ordination. The priest explained how he used to spend hours in vigorous discussion with his youth group, trying to prove the existence of God. The youth leader shook his head and laughed, "We don't waste our time on that these days," he said. "The question kids are asking today is 'Which god?'"

This is a Global Phenomenon

The West is not alone as it confronts this resurgence of spirituality; the same is happening everywhere. A new spiritual hunger seems to be blossoming in every corner of the world, changing the whole way people look at and understand reality. It also leaves them asking a multitude of questions.

St. Alban's Abbey in England was built nearly a millennium ago with bricks unearthed from the ruins of the Roman city of Verulaneum. In 1995 it was the setting for a two centuries' old Church of England tradition, the Church Mission Society's Annual Sermon. The preacher was Josiah Idowu-Fearon, Bishop of the Missionary Diocese of Sokoto in the far northwest of Nigeria, one of those eight missionary dioceses inaugurated by the Nigerian church in 1991 at the beginning of the Decade of Evangelism. He spoke movingly from that ancient pulpit of this extraordinary spiritual hunger, illustrating how universal it is and some of the forms it is taking in Africa.

He told of the reawakening "interest in traditional religion among university students, young business executives, and millions of unreached' tribes," in many parts of Africa today, as further evidence of deep spiritual yearnings. Some of these traditional religions,

Bishop Josiah pointed out, are violently antagonistic to Christianity. He told his listeners that a rising interest in spirituality in any generation is at the same time both a sign of hope, and a warning to Christians not to become lethargic or stumble into syncretism.

With this caveat in mind, one can look almost everywhere today and recognize a quickening interest in the unseen world and in the spiritual. Young Jews, raised in secular homes, are being restored to religious observance and even emigrating to Israel; for them Jewish nationalism is meaningless if it lacks this spiritual and religious dimension. Hinduism is being energized, while, as we have seen, Buddhism is turning itself into a missionary faith, and attracting a growing number of Westerners — including Hollywood stars jaded by Tinseltown's excessive materialism.

Meanwhile, the old paganisms of the West, which many thought were dead and gone, have been revived, given a face lift, and are being marketed with a fresh, fashionable label — The New Age. Often a jumbled hodge-podge of ideas borrowed from pre-Christian Europe, Native American beliefs, the East and modern hedonism, this muddled religious goulash illustrates the hunger and thirst of so many — both young and old — for "something spiritual."[4]

This is not the first time humans have encountered such a smorgasbord. If the pluralism and spiritual hunger of these waning years of the Second Millennium have any parallels, it is with the Roman World into which Christ was born. One reason the Gospel was received so readily in the ancient world was that it spoke to the deepest yearnings of men and women of that time. Could it be that a similar world is being reborn before our eyes, and churches challenged afresh to cultivate this fertile soil? There has hardly ever been a more exciting moment for a Christian to be alive!

With this babble of beliefs jostling for the hearts of humankind, it seems that the Almighty is presenting Christians with opportunities similar to those which made the apostolic and sub-apostolic churches so dynamic. Everywhere, the spiritually hungry yearn to be fed. There is an incompleteness about the world's other great faiths, in addition to something blatantly ersatz about the brand new or revived ancient religions our century has spawned, when they are compared to the Gospel. Meanwhile, there are straws in the wind that God is getting ready to do something new.

These straws fly in from unexpected places — like the Hindu and Muslim worlds. From there come reports which tell of a rapid rise in the number of baptisms due to an unexpected increase in adult conversions to the Christian faith. In one place the number of Christians has grown so much that a worship facility seating 4,500 people and a social services complex are nearing completion. In another place, where there has been a similar explosion of numbers, the government has returned hospitals and encouraged congregations to restore their church building which had been confiscated and desecrated by previous regimes. There is a yearning in the heart of humanity which is reaching epidemic proportions in our time, and the Gospel is the only salve which will satisfy those aching hearts.

A predominant reason for this is that Jesus Christ is not a myth, vision, or figment of someone's imagination. As the Son of God he died on the Cross, is risen and has ascended. Our message is rooted in history and the facts are open to scrutiny to the nth degree by even the most skeptical. "Jesus' bold claim to be the way to God, the truth about God and the very life of God has not been dislodged," writes Michael Green, a priest who is one of those rare mixtures of scholar, theologian, and gifted evangelist. So many of today's religious views are little more than personal ideas, but the Christian message, Green points out, is rooted in fact, stands up under the most intense dissection, while at the same time Christ's resurrection power is experienced by believers and their lives are transformed.[5] There is something extraordinarily all-embracing about Christianity, and in Christ women and men find the wholeness for which they long.

> "Other faiths produce saints from time to time, and that is wonderful. It generally happens after profound searching and meditation and self-discipline on the part of the disciple. But it is the supreme glory of Jesus that he takes all sorts, often from the very cesspools of society, and shows in them the fragrance of his new indwelling life. He, not the disciple, is the main agent at work... Jesus is in the life-changing business. I know whom I have believed, and am not ashamed of the gospel which always has been and still remains the agency of that transformation."[6]

Perhaps the facet of the Gospel which so intrigues those of other faiths is the assurance of sins forgiven. A scholar who recently converted to Christianity from another religion wrote to Cyril that he was not so much converted to a religion, but "captivated by this extraordinary man. Thank you for that book you gave me. It has transformed my life. When I read how a man was being unjustly executed and said of his enemies, Father forgive them...' I said to myself, this man must be God!"

We repeat that it a privilege to be alive at this time, and to be called and empowered by God to share the message of salvation. We have access to the most sophisticated communications system known to humanity to spread the message. In this we are like our first century forebears who used the extensive network of Roman roads to get the message out. In our time we can spread the Gospel using "delivery systems," electronic superhighways, which even a generation ago were in the realms of science fiction.

A Collapse of Ideologies

Another explanation for this extraordinary surge of opportunities is the collapse of what have been dominant global ideologies. Those of us whose youth was over-shadowed by the Cold War could scarcely believe it when the Berlin Wall tumbled down, and then a couple of years later the Hammer and Sickle was hauled down from the Kremlin. In addition, while the People's Republic of China might be a nominally communist country, even privileged Chinese insiders are prepared to admit that Maoism has been hollowed out.[7]

The effects of all this cannot be over-estimated. In North America and Western Europe a massive political realignment is taking place, while almost all Latin America is seriously experimenting with democracy. It is not an exaggeration to suggest the end of civil wars in Portuguese-speaking southern Africa, followed by the relatively bloodless pensioning off of Apartheid in South Africa are phenomena directly related to the end of communism. Now a search is on for alternative systems to interpret life, history, and values. It is no accident that this search is accompanied by an explosion of insatiable spiritual curiosity.

Neither of us are political scientists, so we do not wish to stray far into this territory. However, it is clear that competition is heating up to replace those systems which have dominated the last two centuries. Christian churches have played a significant role in bringing about the collapse of communism, especially in Poland and eastern Germany. Now we are waiting to see if in this ideological vacuum, which will only exist for a relatively short time, Christians are able to recognize the God-given role they are called to play.

New Tools for Communication

While a great deal of the hype surrounding the much-vaunted Internet is just that, it is part of a communications revolution whose potential we have barely started to uncover, let alone exploit. Within a few short years it will be possible to communicate freely from anywhere to anywhere — with the right equipment! A recent photograph in *Time* magazine illustrated this: it showed a herdsman wearing traditional tribal dress somewhere in the heart of Africa. He is talking on his cellular phone while tending his cattle as they graze in the open countryside. Telephones now reach virtually everywhere, and computers are following them into remotest parts at breakneck speed.

A hundred years ago, William Booth, founder of the Salvation Army, echoed John Wesley when he proclaimed that the Devil should not have all the best tunes! Both men saw how important it was to use the resources of their own age to make Christ known — in this case the appropriate musical idiom. As we prepare for the 21st century, perhaps it would be appropriate to ask if we are going to allow the Devil to control all the best technology.

At present, financial traders, marketing entrepreneurs, and academics are plunging into all the possibilities of the emerging system. Alas, when it comes to evangelism Christians have hardly begun to dip their toes in the pool. GEM Research of Richmond, Virginia, points out that those involved in evangelization are only slowly coming online, and "use is lagging far behind that in the business and academic worlds," where more than 6 billion e-mail messages were exchanged in 1993, and that number is growing more than exponentially.[8]

To date, our forays into cyberspace have not been particularly encouraging as far as evangelism is concerned. In fact, the way we use this resource is little more than electronic amplification of past patterns. The Ecunet, a global network used by many churches, is a useful tool to exchange information and to debate issues of the day, but as yet it has been little more than an electronic meeting-place for clergy and lay professionals — dominated by North Americans. The Ecunet helped the pair of us, one in Tennessee, the other in London, to write this book, but its present purpose seems to be of "domestic" service, little thought has been given to making it a more overtly evangelistic tool.

Anglicans are among the most computer savvy Christians in the world, and they certainly have access to the most computers. It is estimated that per head of population, Anglicans are more likely to use computers than any other believers. Yet we have given little thought to ways in which we can employ these tools to tell with relevance "the old, old story." Thoughtful Western observers have noted the cyber-literacy of the young, and point out that unless we learn how to meaningfully use this medium we might lose the opportunity to present Christ to them forever. "Technology is our natural ally."[9]

As people everywhere struggle to unravel life's meaning in this age of spiritual search, is it beyond our imaginations to find ways to provide a practical, relevant apologetic — especially to the young, for whom fast-advancing world of communications wizardry is second nature? As always, Christians are only mastering this fresh medium so they can meet their own needs and chat among themselves. Would that we were so passionate about sharing Christ that we enlisted our ingenuity using it to develop a new apologetic! We have made it like an unwelcoming parish anywhere in the world on a Sunday morning, the faithful talking to the faithful, while ignoring the first time visitors.

As well as providing ways to share the faith, cyberspace is also an environment which can be used to foster prayer and encourage intercession — activities essential to global evangelization. We are amazed how much we have to learn about using this new medium to the glory of God. Maybe one of the great contributions of the North American churches in the immediate future is to share some of its plenitude of computers and communications resources with partners in less privileged parts of the world.[10]

While "talking" through computers may seem horribly impersonal to older generations, people once felt that way about telephones. Yet online conversations could well become the starting point for many as they journey toward faith. We have heard of people being led to faith through Christians willing to experiment with the possibilities of the Internet. As this global network wiggles its way into parts of the world where the Christian faith has until now not been welcome, the possibilities are mind-boggling. Perhaps our slowness to mine this rich vein for the Gospel illustrates our inability to put creativity and imagination into evangelism.

Opportunities Are Everywhere

This is a breathtaking moment in time. The question we must ask ourselves with increasing urgency is how we might capitalize on this array of possibilities? At the moment, windows of opportunity are open, but they will not remain that way forever.

Nigel Scotland is an English priest and college professor who has made some significant studies of the charismatic renewal. In one of his recent books he quoted these sad words by a leader in renewal. "We would have to say in the midst of all this (the charismatic renewal) that we have barely touched the world... We have failed to allow the Holy Spirit to achieve what he wanted, and have instead turned his work in upon ourselves."[11] What is true in renewal circles is probably true of the whole church. We are being challenged to discover imaginative ways to set all our resources loose for the work of witness. It is vital that we break free of past restraints. We must be prepared to let old patterns die so new ones can take their place.

Without doubt, now is the time for the strong, growing, vibrant churches of the global South to grasp the reins of leadership. They need to come to the aid of the struggling churches in the global North, injecting new blood into their tired veins. They must also formulate patterns of ministry which will enable them to reach those who have never heard the Gospel. Meantime, the Northern churches have to discover how to share their more tangible resources with Southern sisters and brothers. Now is the time for advance. God has been preparing us for just this moment!

O Lord Our God,
Who has called us to serve you
In the midst of the world's affairs,
When we stumble, hold us;
When we fall, lift us up;
When we are hard pressed with evil, deliver us;
When we turn from what is good, turn us back;
And bring us at last to your glory. Amen

A Prayer of Alcuin (c735-804)[12]

What we have said:

■ The world is passing through one of the most momentous chapter changes in human history, and all such chapter changes are extraordinary opportunities for Christian witness and mission.

■ The Great Spiritual Depression is over; almost everywhere people are spiritually hungry and are searching.

■ Ancient world religions and newer faiths and cults are swarming onto the global playing field.

■ The collapse of Communism has heralded a time of ideological search and realignment.

■ The Information Revolution has provided us with the most extraordinary tools for witness, evangelism, prayer and Christian ministry if we will but use them.

■ Will we grasp the opportunities or will we drop the ball?

Thinking it over:

■ What is the evidence that we are passing through a major chapter change in human history?

■ Have you seen anything in your community, the attitudes of your friends, family and neighbors, which suggests to you that the Great Spiritual Depression is over? What is your response to this changing situation?

■ How do you think Christians can present their faith in a super-market of religions which includes not only the world's ancient faiths but also a whole array of new religious ideologies?

■ Consider the ways in which the telecommunications revolution might alter your ministry locally and your engagement in evangelism all over the world.

■ What does Paul's approach to the Athenians in Acts 17 have to teach us about the way we approach today's world with the Gospel?

CHAPTER FIVE
From Maintenance to Mission

"All people are called to service in the body of Christ. We need to raise up a new prophetic body who can dream dreams and see visions."
— THE MOST REV. GEORGE L. CAREY
ARCHBISHOP OF CANTERBURY

The Mission Mantra

There is phrase going around Anglican circles these days which is repeated with such extraordinary frequency that it has almost turned into a mantra! The words are "from maintenance to mission." It is being repeated constantly because maintaining the status quo has become so deeply ingrained that in many places mission has been as good as forgotten. We have no objection to this "mantra" because our understanding of ministry has to be jumped out of the maintenance rut. In too many places it is so steeped in the "as it was in the beginning is now and ever shall be" mode, that it is going to take the spiritual equivalent of megatons of TNT to alter the organizing principles of our work.

Around the world, Anglican church life has tended to be modeled on the bucolic parish set in rolling English countryside, and served by a jolly parson who settles down and lives there for ever. This romantic ideal might have been appropriate a couple of hundred years ago when everyone in the locality was at least nominally Christian, but there are few places in the world, especially in England, where this is so today. Not only is the English village an endangered species, but this Christendom approach to ministry has gone the way of the dinosaur.[1]

The problem facing the more established denominations — primarily in the West, but also in other parts of the world — is that they are so soaked in the "care and maintenance" mentality that it will take much more than a "from maintenance to mission" mantra to re-direct their course. Most seminaries and theological colleges spend so much time training pastors, preachers, and even therapists, that evangelism is banished to the kitchen like Cinderella — if it is on the curriculum at all! One diocesan director of evangelism in England complains that, "clergy training is still almost exclusively pastoral and... pays very little attention to evangelistic gifts."[2] The USA is no different, with only one of eleven Episcopal seminaries offering a mandatory course in evangelism. The time is long overdue for sweeping changes in the way we train for ministry, as well as the undergirding principles which shape that training.[3]

The Western churches must pay attention to the outburst of an African bishop who jumped up at the G-CODE gathering and exclaimed that, "Degrees from the UK and the USA are not to do with evangelism... the Western churches have all the theology and nobody gets saved!"[4] He went on to ask whether it was wise for the Two-Thirds World churches to continue sending their brightest and best to the West for further education only to have them come back of little use in a church whose priority is evangelism. We are wondering whether the flow of students might not be reversed — sending them from West to the Two-Thirds World — with the hope of transplanting some African or Asian spiritual enthusiasm into the tired older churches. While no one denies pastoral care is essential to a healthy, holistic ministry, it is like a bicycle with only one wheel without evangelism to complement it — these two facets of ministry belong together.

In Bishop Yong Ping Chung's Diocese of Sabah, evangelism has been made the organizing principle for all they do. If they had not made it so, then in that relatively hostile situation there would be no church at all. Yet the Christians there realized that as exciting as evangelism can be, it is not necessarily easy for ordinary folks. Sabah tries not to lay heavy "guilt trips" on its people, instead teaching their members what they call the 1-1-3 method. What this means is that every worshiper is encouraged to commit to bringing just one person to Christ every three years. They have found that to pray and work toward a modest, but achievable, goal is something which can be reasonably expected of all Christians. It also means that believers can usually focus on someone who is within their existing network of relationships.

And it works! For a number of years now the Diocese of Sabah has grown more than 10% annually. While Bishop Yong Ping Chung shakes his head and admits their progress does not measure up to the ambitious targets set, these are statistics which would lead many a Western bishop to conclude that a full scale revival had broken out![5]

There's Life in the Old Churches Yet!

Despite the gloom which hovers over many Western churches, often to the delight of a predatory media eager to talk up the bad and talk down the good, encouraging things *are* happening. Where there is visionary leadership committed to an honest, biblical faith, a life of prayer, and a focused plan for evangelistic action, God is moving with power. Bishop Yong Ping Chung points out that at the heart of all fruitful evangelism is obedience to the message that God has revealed in Scripture. "We have no high theology," he explains. "We just follow the Bible." As the apostle Peter pointed out to his listeners, God gives his Holy Spirit to those who obey him.[6]

Effective evangelism is not confined to Africa, Asia, or Latin America. We have seen already how the Missionary Diocese of Wakefield has started to turn around, but let's look more closely at the even more astonishing figures coming out of the Diocese of Nelson in New Zealand. In a country where numerical decline has almost been institutionalized as the norm, communicant strength has shot up by 30% during the last five years. Perhaps the driving force behind this expansion is the vision offered by their diocesan bishop, Derek Eaton. With an unwavering biblical faith and a clear idea where the church should go, he is leading his people forward into the evangelistic "Promised Land." Wherever there are *Vision Bearers*, the people are enabled to become "soul harvesters."

God is even at work in the Episcopal Church in the USA, despite the seemingly endless procession of woes which have haunted it, and over which the media have crowed. The audacity of the Bishop of Texas has made fellow-Episcopalians sit up and take notice. On a steaming summer day in 1995, 1,500 Texas

Episcopalians met under a large tent to confer with Claude Payne, their newly installed bishop. The state contains five dioceses and part of a sixth. The Diocese of Texas is the oldest, and includes the oil city of Houston and the capital in Austin. It has a communicant strength of about 74,000.

Even the bishop's closest confidantes had little idea what he would propose when he got up to speak. The most visionary among them had their breath taken away when he announced that he wanted the diocese to work, plan and pray for the diocese to grow to 200,000 by the year 2005 — that is an increase of more than 150% in a decade. Growth like this has not happened in the Episcopal Church since the Victorian era. Bishop Payne's vision draws upon his experience as Rector of St. Martin's, Houston, today one of the largest and most active parishes in North America.

Claude Payne is not the only visionary in the Episcopal Church. In places as diverse as New Mexico, West Missouri, and Pittsburgh new congregations are sprouting in unprecedented numbers; even the tiny diocese of Quincy is getting in on the act. Nevertheless, it is sad to watch dioceses with glorious pedigrees flounder, while in seemingly unlikely spots there is an enthusiasm for mission that has not been seen in generations.

Perhaps one of the most startling American developments is the launching of the North American Missionary Society. Wholeheartedly committed to evangelism and the planting of new congregations, NAMS was able to put four teams of church-planters in place by the end of its first year in operation, while other opportunities are emerging all over the country. Their vision is to plant 1,000 new Episcopal congregations in the next decade. NAMS promises to be an extraordinary and transformatory force in tomorrow's church in America, and is perhaps a model for other countries where the church is struggling. One English visitor to the Episcopal Church has shaken his head as he tried to understand the American church and confessed, "There seems to be the very worst and the very best of Anglicanism side-by-side in the Episcopal Church."

The Younger Generation

Since the time of ancient Greeks, elders have worried about the values and lifestyle of the young. The 1990s are no exception. From Europe, the Americas and to the heart of Africa, parents and pastors fret over the influences with which the young contend, and the evils with which they must tussle.[7] In much of the West, the old-style church youth group designed to mold nice young church men and women is long since defunct. An array of fresh and different styles of reaching the young are desperately needed. One of the things that most worries Bishop Nigel McCulloch of Wakefield about the demographics of his diocese, is that there are less than 800 teens to be found in all the 250 parishes. If that is not a warning signal that radical change is needed, nothing is.

In many places parachurch ministries have done extraordinarily fine work among the young, laboring to understand the youth culture so as to project the faith into it in a meaningful way. Indeed, because of the nature of the youth culture, working with the young can almost be described as a cross-cultural experience for anyone over the age of about 28. Young people challenge the creativity of the churches to the uttermost. One English youth minister explains, "It is not that young people don't want to become Christians, but that the churches can't handle them when they do."[8] As we have noticed already this is shaping up to be a highly spiritual age all over the world; but in their fear of frightening the young away, many churches have tended to offer them everything but a healthy spirituality. They seem to think that soft-pedaling Christ's claims will make the Gospel attractive — the result is precisely the opposite.[9]

Seldom does a youth minister bring a largely middle-aged crowd, including a sprinkling of dignitaries and bishops, to its feet roaring their approval, but Roy Crowne of British Youth For Christ managed to do just that in North Carolina! Speaking about the challenge of reaching the young before nearly 500 Christian leaders from around the world, he had them urging him on. He outlined the problems facing the young in the West in an engaging manner, pleading with the churches to consider the MTV[10] generation as one of the world's "biggest hidden people groups."

"This generation has no dreams," he told his audience, "Give them a sense of destiny" — something which is integral to the gospel of Jesus Christ. "Give them something to believe in." As the moral and familial fabric of Western society has come unglued, the young are often the innocent victims, so "give them a sense of family." This is a generation which needs moral heroes, yet the media feeds their innate cynicism by presenting them with a strong diet of amoral anti-heroes as role models. Is it any wonder they are tempted to ape the behavior, attitudes and lifestyles of those they see on TV, thinking these are the norm? Roy Crowne is a soft-spoken man, but when he reached the climax of his address his voice had risen to a crescendo. He concluded by urging his listeners above everything else: "Always be there for them... Never give up on them."

The young are quick to spot inconsistency and hypocrisy in the lives of the older generations. They ask for clarity, and for unequivocal answers to life's questions. Perhaps one of the concerns facing the world church is whether we are honestly dealing with the questions they are asking, and whether our lifestyle conforms to the teachings of Jesus Christ as found in Scripture. Kids are quick to spot the difference, and will not throw in their lot with something which looks fake or fabricated. In the years ahead it is obvious that youth ministry has to be a high priority in the Western churches, and not the sort of youth ministry that we were used to in the past.

The Diocese of South Carolina has understood this challenge, and have re-ordered their priorities to make it possible for two dozen of their parishes to engage full-time youth ministers to work with the young. Given that 70-80% of all Christians in the USA commit their lives to Christ before they are 18, this is not only excellent stewardship, but an extraordinarily cost-effective approach to ministry. While South Carolina is busy investing in the future, most other dioceses in the West seem determined to focus their assets on holding on to the past.

More Than a Western Problem

At first glance the alienation of the young seems a peculiarly Western challenge, but it is not. Even if generational wars seem endemic only in the West, within a few years these same anxieties about the young are likely to have found their way into the families and churches of Christians in much of the rest of the world. The reason is that the youth culture which is pouring out of North America and Europe today is being gobbled up by the young in every corner of the planet.

It once took months for music or fashions to find their way around the world. Satellites beam styles and sounds from Los

Angeles, New York, London, or Tokyo to anywhere in a nanosecond today, so what's cool in the San Fernando Valley of Southern California, will be cool on the streets of Nairobi or New Delhi tomorrow! Ugandan Christian leaders are concerned that the young in their capital, Kampala, seem captivated by the styles of the Americans who appear on the country's increasing number of television channels. Traditional Ugandan ways, including a healthy social morality and a sense of family, are being abandoned, alas, in favor of the darker side of the American dream.. The communications revolution which is busily at work linking the world's computers, is also enabling the media to get their products to the world's remotest corners — and young men and women who are still trying to forge their identity are a huge potential market, therefore are usually the prime target.

Both in terms of volume and dollar income, popular culture is second only to aircraft as America's major export industry. Futurist John Naisbitt tells us: "America's popular culture is overwhelmingly dominant in the global lifestyle department."[11] Through music, movies, television, publications, and ever-ubiquitous advertising, a secular consumer message is being pumped out to all the world. The idea is that you are what you buy, and the young provide vendors of everything from blue jeans to CDs with a voracious market. Once hooked, marketers hope they will be conditioned to buy much, much more in the years ahead — and as it is all new to them, kids in the Two-Thirds World are far less resistant to the siren song of the advertisers than their Western counterparts.

Churches in areas which are just starting to receive this materialistic and secularizing bombardment are kidding themselves if they think they are immune from the resulting spiritual corrosion. They would be wise to focus now on the struggles of the European and North American churches. The failures of the West could provide valuable lessons for those seeking to present Christ elsewhere.

Normal Beale is a missionary working high in the Himalayas. Not many years ago, the Nepalese community in which he lives was electrified. His neighbors now have an enormous satellite dish and their children watch MTV and other such television offerings. There seems no way to escape such influences. Across the world, the Pacific nation of Fiji's government, alarmed at the influence of American television, banned the broadcasting of all but a few hours of news and current affairs. Their scheme backfired because imaginative entrepreneurs found a way around this censorship by importing videos of everything the government did not want the people to see! Soon these same programs and movies will come along the telephone lines which no one can control, courtesy the Internet.

If the churches are to be effective evangelistically, it is vital that they understand not just today's culture in their region, but also the global culture which is surging in to modify and re-shape it. The same media tools which can communicate the faith effectively where there has been little Christian witness, are also conveying a far less wholesome message, profoundly influencing lives everywhere. The backdrop against which the Western churches have sought to minister in the last two or three generations, will offer the same profound challenge to Christians everywhere.

The resulting weakness of the Western churches stands as a warning. As the worst of secular culture floods out as TV signals — or via the Internet — its spirit-deadening influence cannot but make the Christian task more difficult. It is not even a grain of comfort that other religions are challenged by secularity in exactly the same way. To be forewarned is to be forearmed. The task facing us is to understand its nature and effects, and to develop a full-blooded apologetic which is able to contest its most corrosive effects. If we fail to do that, then much of the progress the churches have made in the last generation could be in jeopardy.

The Rise of Islam

A theme which refused to go away at the G-CODE gathering was the recognition that Islam is a growing force which *has* to be reckoned with everywhere. We have noticed already that Islam has taken root in Britain following massive immigration from Asia, and is now reaching out evangelistically to the indigenous population. The same is true in other places. Today there are more Muslims in the United States than there are Episcopalians and they have made considerable advances into the African-American community. France, with its strong Arab population as a base and its history of secularity, has long been a cherished target of Islamic mission.

Self-confident and backed by petro-dollars, Muslim communities around the world have more than adequate resources to go head-to-head with Christianity. When an Islamic university opened near Mbale, Uganda, in the early 1990s, it could afford faculty salaries far above those being paid at the much respected Makerere University in Kampala. Through this and other educa- tional institutions the Muslims are establishing themselves as an even more potent force in black Africa. Their aim is to entice the rising generation of leaders into their fold. Young Islamic men are actually rewarded for marrying Christian women, having children by them, and then raising these boys and girls as Muslims. There are financial inducements for Muslim men to marry the daughters of Christian clergy — the more important the pastor is the greater the sum paid. Bishop's daughters carry a high premium! These are superficial illustrations, perhaps, but they tell something about the momentum Islam is gathering.

Muslims do not separate "church" and state; Islam is a unity. Put simply, Islam is more than a system of beliefs which adherents attempt to live out within an indigenous culture, hoping through their witness to transform that culture. On the contrary, Islam is a total way of life, beliefs, and practices which are contained in a dis- tinct cultural package — accept Mohammed's message and a com- plete cultural, political, and social framework comes with it. Whereas Christianity "expands from its initial cultural base and is implanted in other societies primarily as a matter of cultural iden- tity... Islam... carries with it certain inalienable cultural assump- tions, such as the indispensability of its Arabic heritage in Scripture, law, and religion."[12]

When Muslims look at the West they do not see a secular world within which a minority church proclaims Christ. Instead they are inclined to interpret the "Christian" world through their own cul- tural presuppositions. As Western culture becomes increasingly global, they see it encroaching on their turf. Many, especially those at the extreme end of the spectrum, tend to view it as a "Christian" tool bent on destroying them, or at least stopping them dead in their tracks. They point to the moral decay of the West, the decline of the family, and the gross inequalities in Western society, laying all these problems at the door of an ane- mic faith. Such representations can make the simple purity of Islam appear extremely appealing — even to Westerners.

If Christians, in this increasingly pluralistic world, are going to move from maintenance to a more dynamic missionary approach, then how we encounter, debate and challenge the presuppositions of Islam must figure prominently in our thinking, praying and strategies. Bernard Lewis of Princeton University, when reviewing the relationship between Europe and Islam since the Muslim faith emerged following the death of Mohammed in the 7th century, says this of the integration of Islamic immigrants into the populations of most major European nations:

> "These communities are still bound by a thousand ties of language, culture, kinship, as well as religion, to their countries of origin, and yet, inexorably, are becoming integrated in their countries of residence. Their presence, and that of their children and grandchildren, will have incalculable but certain immense consequences for the future both of Europe and of Islam."[13]

There is both promise and threat in these words, and what is true for Europe must also be true for those other parts of the world where Muslims have settled.

Anglicanism has more than its share of deeply committed Christians who have become scholars and respecters of Islam and its genius. In many parts of the Islamic world Anglican chaplaincies are the only Christian churches allowed to exist. In such circumstances, the Anglican Communion could have a crucial role to play in the sensitive dialogue between Christianity and Islam. Bishop Kenneth Cragg, perhaps the most knowledgeable of Anglican Islamicists, has said that for all his respect for Islam, what it lacks is a means of atonement and forgiveness. The bishop regards this as the great watershed between Christianity and Islam.[14]

Islam is Just One Ideology Among Many

As we have pointed out, despite the aggressiveness of secularism there is a rising tide of spiritual eagerness worldwide. Any church whose commitment is merely to maintenance will not survive the competition of this open market place of beliefs and ideologies. There is a whole array of new and old religious systems, cults, and even darker religious forces organized and beginning to give the Church catholic a run for her money. That such forces are mustering could perhaps be interpreted as evidence that we are really on the threshold of something extraordinary — and very exciting.

Far from considering this a disaster, perhaps we should look upon it as an unparalleled opportunity. The jostling emergence of a plethora of spiritualities, especially in the West, is evidence that the pillars of a culture erected on Enlightenment foundations are crumbling.   While we have gained much as this culture has evolved, there are many facets of it which have deeply scarred the Christian faith. There is likely to be a time lag while the broader culture catches up with this reality, and then *if we are ready* the opportunities to present Christ could be unprecedented. Churches which refuse to accept the possibilities of this missionary challenge, should ask themselves if they deserve to survive. As Archbishop Carey told his audience at G-CODE 2000, not only are such churches disobedient, perhaps they have forfeited the right to be called churches at all.[15]

Those who are prepared to alter radically their *modus operandi*, turn to God in obedient and believing prayer, teach their members the fundamentals of the faith and how to present these time-honored biblical truths to those outside, and who are willing to go out graciously and engage the forces which are at play, will be the ones who see great blessing.   In short, those who in the power of the Holy Spirit grasp the opportunities and challenges of our time in the "spirit of holiness," will like those who sow in tears (of prayer and hard work), come home, bringing in the sheaves of a great harvest.[16]

Thank God for the mantra that we must move from maintenance to mission. May it stimulate us to make this leap from old to new ways of living out our faith. May the fields produce a harvest which is thirty, sixty, even a hundredfold!

◆◆◆◆◆

O gracious and holy Father,
give us wisdom to perceive you, diligence to seek you,
patience to wait for you, eyes to behold you,
a heart to meditate on you, and a life to proclaim you;
through the power of the Spirit of Jesus Christ our Lord. Amen

(A Prayer of St. Benedict)

What we have said:

■ The constant mantra in many Christian circles today is that the church must move from maintenance to mission.

■ This will require visionary leadership, a willingness to abandon the English village church as our model, and the growth of leadership that is evangelistically minded.

■ Church leaders must become vision bearers and prophets, shifting away from being chaplains and maintenance women and men.

■ One of the greatest challenges facing the churches today is how we reach out to the young, and how we attempt to present the Gospel into youth culture.

■ The secularity of the youth culture is, because of today's communications revolution, no longer just a problem of the West but of all Christians.

■ As grass roots Christianity becomes more missionary-spirited, it is going to find itself facing off with an increasingly virile Islam.

■ Islam is just one of many ideologies in today's "religious marketplace."

Thinking it over:

■ How do you think moving from maintenance to mission as the primary organizing principle would alter the way your congregation functions?

■ Give some consideration to the viability of the Diocese of Sabah's 1-1-3 policy in your congregation or diocese

■ You may not like the music, the clothes, the vocabulary, the style of the young, but how do you think we can best reach out to them?

■ Consider the implications of the global communications revolution. Do you think Christians have a responsibility to preserve cultures which are likely to be destroyed by the imposition of a global culture which is predominantly American? If so, how do we approach this challenge?

■ Pool what you know about Islam. When you have gathered your information, do you think it is enough to be able to present Christ meaningfully to a Muslim friend?

CHAPTER SIX

What's Happening, Where, and How?

"Evangelism means sharing the Good News and the Good News is Jesus Christ." — An Anglican Priest and Evangelist from Southeast Asia

Encouragements

Perhaps the most exciting aspect of attending a large evangelism conference is being able to listen to people talking about the wonderful things God is doing all over the world, and the fascinating way different Christians are approaching the challenge of making Christ known. Conferees may arrive feeling jaded, travel-weary, exhausted from hard work and some of ministry's inevitable disappointments, perhaps wondering why they did not stay comfortably at home. Yet when the gathering is over, they are energized. They leave with a new song on their lips, and fresh prayers of commitment issuing from their hearts.

For those anxious and suspicious about what it means for churches to make the enormous shift from maintenance to mission, stories of church growth elsewhere encourage us to be adventurers, prepared to break the old mold. But it has to be genuine growth! As Bishop Dinis Singulane pointed out when he spoke in North Carolina, there really is a profound difference between a church which really grows because Christ is being proclaimed, and people are being found by God and one which merely swells! A swollen church, he continued, is rather like a church which suffers from elephantiasis!

In the Wake of War

Dinis Singulane turned thirty on the very day he was elected bishop of Lebombo, Mozambique. When he was consecrated he was the youngest bishop in the Anglican Communion. A number of years later he is still one of the younger bishops. When he became bishop his country was in the midst of civil war, congregations had little opportunity to function normally, and believers had often been scattered to the four winds.

In human terms, the challenges facing this young, inexperienced church leader should have crushed him. Yet he never lost heart. When the war was still in full swing he helped the churches work for peace, both by taking active steps to encourage dialogue between the competing factions, and also by praying, fasting, promoting Bible study and teaching about peace, reconciliation, and related issues. In certain places, the diocese even organized marches of witness against the fighting. Refugee camps almost always became centers for ministry, which meant that when refugees were able to return home, or were forced by advancing hostility to move on to another camp, they took their faith with them. The outcome was two churches: one at the new camp and one at the place from which they had come. It was an extraordinary time; the war was terrible, but as Christians were obedient to God, it became a catalyst for growth!

Today, with peace once more restored, Mozambique, one of the world's least affluent nations, is picking itself up following this long and disastrous interlude in its life. As it does so, the bishop and his diocese are moving forward enthusiastically with the Gospel. Numerical growth is just one end product in a church wholeheartedly committed to evangelism, and should never be the sole reason for evangelistic ministry. A church which is evangelistic is not one whose pews are packed, rather it is a congregation which not only welcomes the outsider, but also employs all its gifts and resources to introduce people to Jesus Christ, died and risen, translating the message into terms that they can understand. Evangelistic churches everywhere in the world usually expect a high level of commitment from their members, set challenging but attainable goals, and tend to be warm, welcoming, and compassionate communities.

Bishop Singulane told his audience in North Carolina how his wife sometimes asks him to bring perfume home for her when he leaves Mozambique for trips overseas. This means that when he smells a fragrance he likes and thinks she will enjoy wearing, he is eager to find out where he can get it to take home as the gift she wanted. Evangelism, he muses, should be like a sweet perfume. "If our evangelism is so fragrant, then even if people don't know about it, they'll ask us where they can get it." This kind of leadership has put evangelism is at the very top of the agenda in the diocese — which includes most of the huge country of Mozambique, bordering the Indian Ocean in south-eastern Africa.

Almost inevitably, where there is dynamic evangelistic ministry, those evangelizing have set themselves measurable targets — Mozambique is no exception. For example, 1993 was the centenary year of Anglicanism in their country. To celebrate they committed to establish 100 new congregations, challenged each congregation to sell 100 bibles in their community, and to present 100 new believers for baptism and/or confirmation. They also encouraged each Christian to speak to 100 others about Jesus Christ. Because of their concern for the environment, which had been so badly damaged during the war, each congregation was to plant 100 trees in order to show God's love for creation. While not everyone may have reached their targets, this approach accelerated growth.

Even the end of hostilities provided an opportunity for evangelistic witness within the context of public penitence. Led by the bishop, a band of Christians went on a 1,000km pilgrimage which wound its way right across the country, stopping in villages where there had been massacres to tell the story of the Prince of Peace. In each of these places they performed the Stations of the Cross, interspersing them with bible readings, a presentation of the Gospel, and followed up with a call to repentance and forgiveness. This act of penitence, a symbolic attempt to release people from the effects of brutality and violence, left in its wake havens where healing is taking place, and the quality of life is being transformed.

The evangelistic example of the bishop obviously counts. Dinis Singulane takes seriously his call as Chief Evangelist. One day he found himself sitting beside a small girl on a flight from Maputo, Mozambique, to Johannesburg, South Africa, to pick up an intercontinental connection. During that flight he not only introduced the child to Jesus Christ, but had the pleasure of seeing her then go and perch herself beside a woman who looked downhearted, and tell her of the love of Christ. This says something for the passion for evangelism which reaches outward from one bishop who has come to understand his episcopal calling to be priest, prophet, pastor, preacher, and evangelist. "The Gospel is so exciting," he admits, "that we cannot but speak of what we have heard or seen regarding Jesus Christ."

Despite the grinding poverty of Mozambique, the diocese sees evangelism not just as a local, but also as an international business. It has already launched its own missionary activity in the other Portuguese-speaking countries in Africa. Angola, itself struggling to find stability in the wake of a brutal civil war, has already become an archdeaconary under the pastoral care of Bishop Singulane. There are now 20,000 Anglicans there. Bishop Singulane and his people are praying and working toward many more Angolans coming into the Kingdom of God through their church before the turn of the millennium — and the signs look good. Mozambique might culturally be at the opposite ends of the spectrum to most Western churches, yet there is much other Christians can learn from Mozambican zeal and priority setting.

Anglican Growth in Chile

Latin America has always been something of a step-child in the Anglican Communion. Anglicans have been working there for several centuries, either in English-speaking chaplaincies or focused upon some of the native peoples. In Northern Argentina, Paraguay, and Southern Chile, missionaries from the South American Missionary Society planted the roots of the faith deep in the hearts of native peoples like the Mataco and the Mapuche. In the last quarter century, they also played a major role enabling these tribes to maintain their identity in the face of the onslaught of development. In the Southern Cone of South America , Anglican work did not properly begin in the cities until about 25 years ago.

While missionary work undertaken from Britain, Australia, and New Zealand has been at the heart of church planting efforts in the south of the continent, it was from North America that Anglican Christianity came to Brazil, the northern tier of republics, and Central America. Progress has been patchy, but from all corners of Latin America come increasing examples of effective evangelism, especially in the continent's burgeoning cities and among the emerging middle classes.

Patricio Browne is a burly, friendly man with an enormous beard. He pastors a congregation in La Reina, a growing suburb of upwardly mobile people in Chile's increasingly prosperous capital of Santiago. Patricio's parents and grandparents moved to Chile early in this century from various European countries. His congregation, planted in early 1994, evolved in an 18 month period from a group of 40 people meeting in a home, to a fellowship of more than 150 who have developed the alarming habit of growing out of their meeting space — which happened to be a converted family house when we talked to Patricio. One of the problems facing him when he returned home to Chile from the USA was this accommodation dilemma. Children's and family ministries which were developing in encouraging ways, would soon be terribly hampered by the squeeze on space, and this work would be crucial for the congregation's life as the Chilean summer approached.

The La Reina congregation is an off-shoot of the parish in the Las Condes neighborhood, itself now a 800-900 member church. It, too, started in a home some twenty years earlier. These congregations are symbolic of what is happening in a diocese which until the 1960s worked almost exclusively with indigenous peoples. Today the Diocese of Chile has nearly one hundred congregations, and is exploring new opportunities in parts of the country where there has been little or no Anglican work. Church-planting is vital for the steady expansion of the Chilean church, again a lesson that the older churches in the global North need to re-learn if they are to have a healthy future.

Like the church in Mozambique, Chileans also have a global vision. Several years ago they sent an evangelistic team back to the Old World, to Spain. Out of this relationship came the vision to bring their Chilean enthusiasm to the tiny, and once fearfully persecuted, Reformed Episcopal Church in Spain. Today there are four Chileans working with the Spanish church in evangelistic and church-planting ministries.[1] More Chileans are likely to follow in their footsteps. It is no accident that wherever in the world there are healthy churches, they have a strong and glowing commitment to the global spread of the Gospel.

Again, like Mozambique, one of the keys to church growth and evangelistic enthusiasm has been the bishop, Colin Bazley, a person with a large vision and feisty determination. Like Dinis Singulane, he is not a glorified church bureaucrat but a chief evangelist convinced that evangelism should be more than the "ghetto activity" of a handful of enthusiasts, but that every facet of a diocese's life should be evangelistic. By the mid-1990s, Bishop Bazley, one of the longest serving diocesans in the Anglican Communion, had led the diocese through several chapters of its development. His long tenure illustrates how strategically important it is for leaders to hang in for the long haul — and in a country like Chile, stable leadership has been vital.

> "We have a volatile society here and people live on their emotions," Bishop Bazley writes. "It is not difficult to get a decision to 'let Jesus into your life,' 'make Jesus Savior' or 'accept salvation.' It is very difficult to produce stable disciples who, by God's grace, persevere, with Christ exercising His lordship in every area of their lives. Indeed, biblical reformed Christianity is so new and little known that people coming to a living faith often have no idea of the demands this will involve. No religion they have known before in their experience has asked for such ethical consistency."[2]

An New Kind of Initiative in Honduras

Honduras in Central America is another diocese in which God is doing extraordinary things as a result of strong and visionary leadership. Twenty years ago about the best word to describe the Diocese of Honduras was "minuscule." Two decades later it is experiencing considerable expansion because of the foresight of their former bishop, Hugo Pina, and for the last dozen years, that of Leopoldo Frade. The diocese now has more than fifty congregations and preaching stations, and also exercises social and education ministries through Episcopal schools, clinics, and two orphanages — one for boys, and one for girls. Both Leo Frade, and his wife, Diana, are strong, energetic, and visionary leaders.

Perhaps one of the most fascinating church-planting experiments by Anglicans in Latin America is now well underway in the Honduran capital of Tegucigalpa. Patterned after an approach pioneered by the Christian and Missionary Alliance Church (CMA) in Peru in the 1970s, the mission congregation of Cristo Redentor, was launched in 1992. The target population is unchurched middle and upper middle class Hondurans. Led by a team of a dozen missionaries sponsored by the South American Missionary Society[3], its intention from the beginning has been to have 1,000 members within ten years, to be financially self-supporting, and at that point to be ready to launch a daughter congregation which bears the same "genetic imprint." It is the intention of both diocese and founders that by that time, 100% of the leadership will come from within the congregation.

By mid-1995, three years after its start, the worshipping congregation on any given Sunday was around 170, and Colombian priest, Juan Bernardo Morentes, who is now Vicar, is encouraged by progress. Such strategies are not without their problems, but barring crises, Cristo Redentor looks set to reach its goals by the turn of the century. This "Abundant Life" approach to church-planting, which the CMA pioneered in several Latin countries and now among Spanish-speakers in Miami, Florida, fits the Anglican ethos well, and could probably be transferred into a variety of other cultural settings. It is much more than the sophisticated "head-hunting" operation that its critics claim. Its intention is to lead outsiders to faith, build them up to maturity in Christ, meanwhile equipping them for ministries which are evangelistic, pastoral, or social and humanitarian. Abundant Life congregations in Colombia, Peru, and Argentina, have not only established, but also fund from their own treasures an array of congregationally-based ministries designed to serve less fortunate neighbors.

One of the keys to the early success of La Iglesia de Cristo Redentor was the months of prayer and team-building which laid a foundation for the work before ever they began reaching out into the community. Time and again, as we have seen God at work and as we have listened to people's stories, we realize that a commitment to intercessory and repentant prayer is at the heart of all successful evangelistic strategies. This does not preclude careful organization and management, but is absolutely vital if the work organized is to have a profound impact. The greatest temptation everywhere is to reduce the time spent on our knees, increase self-gratifying activism, and then hope this will precipitate change at little personal cost!

A New Diocese in Tanzania

Nowhere is the priority of prayer known better than in Tanzania. In May 1991, Alpha Mohammed resigned as Bishop of the Diocese of Mount Kilimanjaro near the Tanzanian border with Kenya, and traveled south to the region where he grew up. A month later the new Diocese of the Rift Valley was inaugurated, and Bishop Alpha installed as bishop. The day was a gala occasion with the Prime Minister, various cabinet ministers, and eleven bishops in attendance to launch this new venture. And *venture of faith* is exactly what it was.

Having left a comfortable home and established diocese focused around the beautiful city of Arusha, the Mohammed family found themselves in a diocese which had no money, no office, no telephone, no house for the bishop, no vehicles, no cathedral, and 25 pastors spread out over a vast area ministering in some 20 scattered parishes. Like most houses in Manyoni, the new "see city," the home in which they settled had no electricity, and there was just one small vestry room in the local church, which the bishop could use as an office — and the only office equipment was a table and a chair!

Early on, the new diocese received some modest financial gifts from friends and well-wishers, enabling Bishop Alpha to hire himself a secretary and fund the ministry of a priest who knew the territory well, and who could take responsibility for evangelistic work. His small team in place, they gave themselves to the work of intercessory prayer. Each day they would meet in the church to pray before the office work began, and they would pray together at the end of the working day. Their prayers were fervent but simple. First, that the Lord would call people to himself from all over the diocese, and that he would raise up teams committed to mission and evangelism. Second, that God would give them wisdom as they sought to discern the right strategy.

One of their earliest encouragements was visitors from the USA. Christians came from the Diocese of Colorado, Truro Church in Fairfax, Virginia, and the Church of All Angels in the heart of New York City. They came to encourage and they came to bring help. In the months that followed things began to shape up. After much striving, by mid-1995, the bishop finally had a home, and there was a fine new administrative building for the diocese and its outreach ministries. Meanwhile, in the heart of Manyoni, beside the old St. Matthew's Church where the bishop had set up his first office, a new cathedral seating 1200 people is starting to take shape.

Bricks and mortar are mere symbols of the work God is doing in the Diocese of the Rift Valley. When the G-CODE gathering took place, it had already grown from those humble beginning to 147 congregations in 31 parishes, ministered to by 44 ordained pastors, and a growing team of evangelists and catechists. There were "only" 39,000 communicants when Bishop Alpha arrived in 1991, four years later that number has increased by 20,000 and is gathering pace daily. The prayers in which the new diocese has been doused from the outset, continue to be lifted heavenward each day. These intercessions are being answered as nominal Christians find a living faith, and the Gospel makes an impact on the lives of the animist and Muslim majority in the region.

Alpha Mohammed is a self-effacing and intensely humble man — he also has an infectious sense of humor. Reared in a Muslim home, he was converted to Christ when a teenager. His own evangelistic ministry has been an inspiration to Christians the world over. God has used him over the years to bring tens of thousands to a living faith. He has already imprinted his own extraordinary gifts into the life of his young diocese: prayer and an on-going strategy for evangelization being his highest priorities.

Literacy is widespread in Tanzania, despite the country's poverty. The Central Tanganyika Press, the Church of the Province of Tanzania's publishing house, produces as much Christian literature as it can with its limited resources.[4] Books and pamphlets are literally "devoured" by those who can get hold of them as soon as they come off the presses. Bishop Alpha chairs its board. The reason for his commitment to this work is simple: he wants Tanzanian Christians to do more than just make decisions to follow Christ. As most of them can read, he wants them to have books, bibles and study aids to help them to deepen their faith. This Tanzanian Christian leader realizes that if there is to be an on going renewal of hearts, then minds must also be renewed, and renewed minds require a strong diet of healthy literary food.[5]

What Do We Learn From These Examples?

These stories from Africa and Latin America are but a small

sample of Anglican evangelistic activity, yet each illustrates the importance of the vision of Christian leaders. Every bishop we have mentioned is committed to evangelistic ministry, and looks for that same commitment among his clergy and lay leadership. Making evangelism a priority is the task of a chief evangelist, even if that particular bishop does not personally have strong evangelistic gifts. Bishops Mohammed and Singulane have strikingly obvious gifts of evangelism, whereas Bishops Bazley and Frade use their skills as teachers, dreamers, visionaries, and organizers, more as agents of evangelism — although each is eager to share his love for Christ with unbelievers when the opportunities present themselves.

The call to evangelism is in fact a call to the whole people of God — beginning with the leadership. Churches function best when their bishops model this Gospel imperative. The late Bishop of West Malaysia, Tan Sri Savarimuthu, whose diocese experienced such tremendous growth after his own "conversion," asserted that, "The Holy Spirit is brooding over us to grant us fresh anointing, not only to the bishop, clergy, and lay workers, but to all of us.[6]

Churches which have been established for a long time, tend to raise to leadership those with many extremely important gifts, but sadly, evangelism and outreach are seldom at the top of these leaders' agenda. When this happens it is hardly surprising that other priorities assert themselves, and the evangelistic vision, with all the hard work and sacrifice it demands, ebbs away to be replaced by the maintenance mentality.

This has happened in the West, and it threatened the Church in Nigeria a generation ago. The slide toward nominalism was halted by renewal in Nigeria, and now a younger generation of leaders has restored the vision to move outward into all the world. The result is that today the Anglican Church in Nigeria has 11 million members, and is not only the largest church in the Anglican Communion, but is also one of the most dynamic and fast-growing. There have certainly been tensions as the Nigerian church has steered away from the easy course of least resistance, managing change is never easy. We can expect something similar to happen wherever Christians place evangelism at the top of their list of priorities.

The lesson of these churches we have highlighted is that Christians must exercise great care as they set aside leadership. The bishop's primary job description ought to be Chief Evangelist, which means that person's previous ministry should demonstrate either experience as an evangelist, or evidence that evangelism and mission are at the heart of their previous work. Overtly evangelistic bishops understand the power of prayer, and are able to develop strategies with measurable goals and objective. Maintenance merely keeps the old machinery going. That will not do in the world which is emerging as the Second Millennium fades away.

O Lord God,
when thou givest to thy servants to endeavor any great matter,
grant us also to know that it is not the beginning,
but the continuing of the same unto the end,
until it be thoroughly finished, which yieldeth the true glory;
through him who for the finishing of thy work laid down his life,
our Redeemer Jesus Christ. Amen

(A Prayer of Sir Francis Drake)

What we have said:

■ There is a difference between genuine church growth and swelling.

■ The role of the diocesan bishop as the Chief Evangelist is vitally important to the healthy evangelistic ministry of the church.

■ Stability of leadership is important to the long-term health of a diocese or parish as it grows.

■ Successful church-planting and evangelistic ministry are rooted and grounded in prayer.

■ When work spreads outward, like the Diocese of the Rift Valley, it is a venture of faith.

■ We need to exercise great care in the people we call to be our leaders.

Thinking it over:

■ Discuss what you think the difference is between growing and swelling.

■ Is it easier to plant new congregations in a country like Chile than to plant them in places where Anglican or Episcopal churches have been in existence far longer? If so, why?

■ Think about the relationship between church planting and prayer, looking particularly at La Iglesia de Cristo Redentor in Tegucigalpa.

■ Look at the qualifications for leadership that the early church sought in Acts Chapter 6. Do these apply today, and if so why?

CHAPTER SEVEN

The Rich Evangelistic Tapestry

"Making disciples is a command to be obeyed, not just an issue to be discussed at conferences."
— THE RT. REV. YONG PING CHUNG, BISHOP OF SABAH

It is amazing how often evangelistic ministry is hampered by our unwillingness — or inability — to be creative and to minister with imagination. Not long ago someone suggested, slightly tongue in cheek, that almost all the churches in the USA seemed to have surrendered most of their creative juices to the Walt Disney organization! Tangible evidence of this is easy to find, both in the US and the rest of the world. For example, whenever a parish, diocese, or parachurch organization does something that works, everyone jumps onto the bandwagon, mindlessly attempting to replicate it. Sometimes we seem incapable of extricating principles from such successful strategies, and then seeing how best they can be adapted to our situation. Forgetting that God's Holy Spirit is always the unseen and uncontrollable ingredient, it seems we are always out looking for that one surefire "how-to" recipe for success.

We have already determined that there are common threads that shape the ministries of growing congregations and dioceses around the world. But, if we look carefully at each of them you discover that each undertakes evangelism differently, because they are sensitively dependent on the nature of their environment. In this chapter we will be looking at some ways Anglicans are being evangelistically successful around the world. Christians in

Malaysia or Melanesia may have found a helpful model that can be replicated in other parts of the world, but these models are to be learned from, not slavishly imitated. This is what it means to respond to the Holy Spirit within our own context, in a style and "language" of the place where we find ourselves.

One of the major characteristics of evangelistic, apostolic churches is this: instead of expecting people to come looking for them, they go out seeking potential new Christians themselves. The prevailing culture in the Western churches, having been at the heart of a community for hundreds of years, expects that when folks have spiritual needs they will make a bee-line for our doors. Behind this assumption is the misguided belief that Christianity is still "the only show in town." Because we have habitually thought this way for so many generations, we often seem incapable of realizing that particularly since World War II a huge "stained glass barrier" has grown up between our ecclesiastical world and the vast majority. This obstacle now blocks the threshold over which we want people to venture in most instances.

This is a prime example of how the old way of doing things no longer works. In most places, the old paradigm has all but dissolved, we must now take the initiative and go out "into the highways and byways" when introducing people to Jesus Christ — their Savior and ours — wherever they happen to be. While this might require more hard work and ingenuity on our part, we might be startled by the results. When we confine our God to the inside of church buildings, how can we expect believers to exhibit a true Christian character in the workplace, for example?

One-on-One Witness

At the heart of the evangelistic enterprise everywhere is the manner Christians live out their faith. It is their actions and words that draw others to Christ, in the home, at work, or even on the baseball triangle, the cricket field, or the soccer pitch. An outsider might meet Christ with the sudden-ness of Paul on the Damascus Road, but more often it is a gradual process, sometimes as imperceptible as the growth of a tree. However it happens, coming to Christ is the human response to God's grace working through the words, actions, and prayers of believing people.

The basic building block of the church's evangelistic life is faithful people sharing their convictions with others — like the middle-aged woman mentioned earlier, who talked with her mother as they sat in the car on a quiet London side-street. Discerning Christians are as uncomfortable with evangelistic styles which are rude and intrusive as those who might find themselves on the receiving end of such "assaults," but when the faith is shared with the same sensitivity Jesus showed when dealing with the woman at the well in Samaria, the results can be extraordinary. When evangelism overflows from personal relationships or the sheer quality of a person's life, responding to the message becomes a natural and logical sequence.

Some have the spiritual gift of evangelism,[1] that is, they have the innate capacity to be the channels through which God leads vast numbers into his Kingdom. Church growth studies in recent years have concluded that in any one congregation as many as 10% of all believers have this specific gift, equipping them to spearhead evangelistic ministry. That they do not possess this gift does not excuse the majority from the responsibility of living out their faith, and sharing the hope within them. Many of those who have been involved in teaching evangelists point out that even those with specific evangelistic gifts need training to be effective and to find confidence in their ministry.

While in Mozambique it might be culturally appropriate to encourage Christians to share their faith with 100 other people in a year, given differing social patterns, such a strategy would be likely to misfire in other parts of the world. However, an adaption of the 1-1-3 strategy of the Diocese of Sabah might be a far more effective way to encourage each "ordinary" Christian to share in the adventure of making new Christians. We hazard a guess that, presented appropriately, 1-1-3 would probably work well in places like the Missionary Diocese of Wakefield; Brisbane, Australia; or Tokyo, Japan. Yet if the bishops in those places were to invite their members to witness to 100 people each year, the resulting stampede in the opposite direction might be as dangerous as shouting "Fire!" in a crowded theatre!

Whatever the setting in which one-on-one evangelism takes place, it will be ineffective if believers do not understand the meaning of salvation, have not experienced it, or are not able to explain how it has changed their lives. The onus is on the clergy and other

Christian leaders to teach, equip and train congregations, so that even those who do not possess strong evangelistic gifts can be faithful Christian witnesses. By exercising just a little bit of imagination, all sorts of ways can be dreamed up to share our faith effectively.

The Evangelism Explosion program for personal witness, developed by Coral Ridge Presbyterian Church in Florida, has been an attractive tool for teaching personal witness in a number of places in the Anglican world,[2] although it has not worked everywhere. While this approach now appears to be past its peak in most places, through it tens of thousands have learned ways to share sensitively with outsiders what it means to be a follower of Jesus Christ. The Alpha Course, which has grown out of the exciting evangelistic ministry of Holy Trinity, Brompton, London, is proving most effective in a growing number of parts of the Western world. It has been an especially effective way of sharing Christ with those from more literate backgrounds. It is just one of a number of evangelistic approaches which present the Gospel within the context of small group relationships.

In the world's cities and megacities, in the West, and among that growing number who receive higher levels of education, people are more likely to be both deeply influenced by secularity, and highly individualistic. These people are less likely to come to faith as part of a group or extended family, but one at a time; they are often led along by a friend or family member, their interest having been aroused by a family occasion like a baptism or even a funeral.

However, there are still many places where people function as members of a larger social grouping. Key individuals must be focused upon, if there is to be an effective evangelistic encounter in these settings. When community leaders decide that following Christ is the right way forward, the whole group comes along as well. We have already noticed that Anglicans working with tribal people in parts of Southeast Asia recognize that the strategic individual with whom they share the faith is the head man. This pattern of group conversion seems to have been the practice of the early church, the clearest example being the coming to Christ of the jailer's household in Philippi.[3]

Preaching

American evangelist Billy Graham is the acclaimed twentieth

century master of evangelistic preaching, although there are many others God uses in the same way. The late Bishop Festo Kivengere from western Uganda was often dubbed "The African Billy Graham." Today Bishop Festo's mantle seems to have fallen on the shoulders of men like Bishops Alpha Mohammed and Dinis Singulane. Priests like Nigeria's Chinedu Nebo and England's Michael Green have pointed the way for many, while Chile's, Alfredo Cooper has been extraordinarily used by God in Latin America.

In a number of places, going out with a well-planned and prayed over mixture of preaching, teaching, music, dance, and drama, is proving remarkably effective. This is Alfredo Cooper's forte. He has preached in the open air in Santiago using a variety of visual aids to illustrate his point and engage the minds of those listening to him. Across the ocean in England, as part of the Archbishops' Springboard for Evangelism, scholar and evangelist Michael Green relishes opportunities to preach in the open air. Whenever possible he is accompanied by a team of gifted actors, musicians, even dancers.

This is a little like returning to the morality plays of the Middle Ages, which were such a popular spiritual tool, as well as being great entertainment. Perhaps the secret of successful open air preaching is to entertain as well as to engage those who pass by. The same is true of "crusade-style" events. For these to succeed there must be drama, excitement, and a sense of expectation. In less formal public settings there must be give-and-take between preacher and audience. Each of us has preached in the open air, and has learned that handling hecklers can be fun, after the initial shock of being interrupted, helping you to scratch people where they spiritually really are itching.

In many countries, evangelistically-minded parishes regularly hold special services to which members invite their friends, neighbors and family. In the midst of joyful, seeker-sensitive worship, there will be an evangelistic presentation, followed by opportunities for conversation as well as the public profession of faith in Christ. The late Canon David Watson noted that "Christians worshipping together can be a powerful factor in effective evangelism, providing the worship has a note of reality about it with joy inspired by the Holy Spirit."[4] However, evangelists have discovered and rediscovered that all their efforts are more or less in vain if congregations don't pray, and if there is no effort to enfold new believers into the fellowship.

Alas, huge numbers who make a commitment to Jesus Christ tend to slip away in a relatively short time. It is estimated that in England 80% of those who confess Christ are likely to disappear out of the back door of the church within five years, and figures like this can probably be replicated almost everywhere. People whose lives have been affected in this way are likely to be doubly difficult to reach with the Gospel a second time around. Not only does this illustrate the spiritual nature of the battle in which we participate, it also points up the necessity of adequate follow through, turning those who simply profess faith into genuine disciples.

The Importance of Relationships and Small Groups

In the last thirty or forty years there has been a rediscovery around the world of the power of small groups. Initially they tended to be tacked onto the other activities of a congregation, but in an increasing number of places the cell group has pushed itself from the periphery and is now the primary organizing unit of the Christian community. Through the ages, small groups have played an important role in the revival of religion. John Wesley understood their value in the eighteenth century, and "classes" were the lynch pin of the Methodist movement as it spread through rapidly industrializing England — then the world. Alas, the inflexibility of the Church of England prevented the new wine of Methodism from being retained within its ranks.

There has been another veritable explosion of small groups in the last few years, both within and beyond the Christian church. In North America, Alcoholics Anonymous, co-founded by Episcopal priest Samuel Shoemaker, pioneered the scores of self-help groups which provide support through the "Twelve Step Method" for those wrestling with every kind of dysfunction.[5] A Gallup International Institute survey in 1988 yielded the startlingly encouraging information that 21% of all Americans had attended some kind of "prayer group, Bible study, or other religious group which meets somewhere other than a church," during the previous month.[6]

Perhaps the most outstanding example of small groups is in South Korea. The biggest Pentecostal congregation in the world is in Seoul, and began as cell groups led primarily by women, now has a membership estimated at 800,000 — configured in 90,000 small groups. Nowhere can Anglicans match such extraordinary numerical progress in one congregation, yet wonderful tales are coming from small groups everywhere.   In the Diocese of Singapore, for example, a majority of the forty congregations organize themselves around cell groups. These play a significant role both in the outreach and mission of the parish, and in helping new members feel at home.

One of the most exciting small group stories comes from the Diocese of Sabah. The Revd. Albert Vun is Rector of the Anglican Church in Tawau, a seaport city with some 40,000 inhabitants. Each Sunday his church has five services: two in Chinese, two in English, and one in Bahasa Malay. They usually total more than 2,000 worshipers. Key to the health of this congregation is not Sunday worship, but the network of cell groups.

When 1995 began there were 96 cells, but the parish did not expect the roster to stay there for long. They had prayerfully committed to adding 600 new believers in the following twelve months, and were working toward that goal.   On February 10, 1995, they formed their 97th cell. The parish in Tawau does not talk about cells "splitting" or "dividing," believing more organic language is appropriate for the Body of Christ. They prefer to describe cells as *multiplying*. It is their policy that once a group has more than fifteen members the multiplier effect is put into practice.[7]

Small groups provide caring support, but also enable evangelism to take place in a non-threatening setting, like someone's home. In the anonymity of the world's cities, belonging is a treasure for which people long.   Small groups offer such intimacy. People searching after truth can get to know credible Christians, and as they warm to the group, anxieties will subside, and they can ask about Jesus Christ, and other questions which might be troubling them. A small group is a setting within which faith is caught rather than taught. The Rector refers to the new members who are absorbed into the cell groups in Tawau as "open heart" people. He says they are like Lydia, the seller of purple fabrics who St. Paul met in Philippi, because they are open to receive Christ.[8]

Robert Wuthnow of Princeton University has undertaken exhaustive study of the small group phenomenon. He concludes that they flourish where the church is strong, not when it is weak.

Small groups, far from being an alternative to church, are a dynamic extension to the central ministries of a congregation. Where people are lonely and hurting, it appears that a warm, informal environment can provide the Christian nurture which has the power to usher them into the Kingdom of God.

Another American, Carl George, after having analyzed the workings of hundreds of congregations has concluded that cell groups are fundamental to what he calls the *Meta-Church*. They are essential to the *metamorphosis*, or transformation, of congregations, but they are also environments in which people can experience *metanoia*, which is the Greek word meaning repentance and conversion to Christ. He writes that Meta-Churches "have blended evangelism and pastoral care with leadership development in such a way that they win people to Christ as they care for them."[9]

One of the most admired figures in North American Anglicanism in mid-century was Sam Shoemaker.[10] He used to tell people that as much as he admired those who could jump into the heart of the Christian community, his place was by the door. He wanted to be far enough in so he could be "near enough to God to hear Him, and know He is there. But not so far from people as to not hear them — outside the door."[11] Small groups are one of the most effective ways for a multitude of Christians to fulfill this same function, especially when reaching out to those with more introverted personalities. People yearn to meet God, yet because of their humanity, they are more likely to make this encounter through women and men who are neither afraid nor ashamed of their own human-ness.

Healing and Miracles

Healings and miracles seemed part and parcel of the life of the early church, and the miraculous has erupted ever since — sometimes after centuries of apparent quiescence. In our century, stories and experiences of healing and divine intervention have increased. There is a tendency for those of us raised in more rationalistic cultures to look with suspicion upon such things — that is, until something beyond comprehension happens to us or within the context of our ministry. Even if Westerners have severe doubts about the relationship between disease, dysfunction, and the spiritual forces of darkness, Christians in other parts of the world do not share such doubts.

A devout Anglican priest who prefers anonymity because of the pressures on the church in his country, talked to us in guarded terms about his experience of the dark forces which have sought, on various occasions, to wreak havoc in his own extraordinarily effective evangelistic ministry. On one occasion he was preaching an evangelistic sermon when he was literally struck dumb. He learned later that those who wanted to shut him up had stooped to the occult in an attempt to do so. But the grace of God protected him, restoring his voice and intensifying the power of his ministry.

Such stories might still be rare in the developed world, but can be echoed times without number by Christians in other places. We repeat again what we have already said: because evangelism is the cutting edge of mission, the sharpest point of encounter with the world, there is a profound element of spiritual warfare at its heart.

A relatively new congregation in Malaysia, has been established in one of the poorest districts of Kota Kinabalu. Kota Kinabalu is the city at the foot of Mount Kinabalu, the highest peak in Borneo. The congregation has no priest. It was planted and continues to be led by lay people, one of whom is businessman, Ronnie Liew En Khiam. In less than three years this budding Christian community has grown - from two men visiting around a deprived area, praying, and representing Christ to a dubious population, to a thriving assembly of more than 160.

All these new Christians had never even heard of Jesus Christ or understood the loving power of God until they met Ronnie — who introduced them to the Lord. They are mostly of Chinese descent, continually struggling to make ends meet. Through ancestor worship, Ronnie explains, they have remained in spiritual bondage from generation to generation. The occult, witchcraft, and spiritism permeate every facet of their lives, so when there are difficulties it is to these forces that they turn. Sitting in the gentle sunshine of a soft September afternoon in the Smoky Mountains, far from the towering might of Mount Kinabalu, Ronnie explained the spiritual murkiness which envelopes so many lives. He told of how the physically or mentally ill are taken to witch doctors, medicine men, Chinese temples, or one of the mediums who abound in those narrow streets.

He recalled how he met a family whose twelve-year-old daughter was in an extremely depressed state. The parents had tried all the traditionally accepted methods, yet her condition had continued to deteriorate. They were at their wit's end. People would slam their doors when mother and daughter walked by, fearful that the demons which possessed the adolescent would jump into their houses and somehow take over. When they had reached such a state of desperation that they were willing to try anything, someone suggested that they "ask the church to come."

After their first visit, when Ronnie and his companions had sized up the task before them, *they spent several days fasting and praying*, regularly returning to the home and interceding for the troubled child. Ronnie grimaced as he remembered, "It was warfare prayer." It turned out to be a week of fearsome spiritual struggle. Improvement was not dramatic, but after a few days the girl began emerging from this cloud of despair, her spirits slowly lifting. In a relatively short time she returned to school. Today she lives a perfectly normal life, and Ronnie assured us that she has a delightful disposition and a fine self-image. Ronnie knows this because he sees her every week at church.

The girl's healing was not the end of the tale. This experience had a profound impact on the whole extended family, who realized they had come face to face with a deity whose power and compassion were greater than anything they had ever seen. Today this clan of four nuclear families has come to Christ. At their baptism they destroyed their charms and amulets, becoming vibrant communicant members of the Body of Christ. Ronnie could have talked for hours about the healings and miracles he has seen as they planted this congregation. As a result of the tenacity of Ronnie and his companion in that tumble-down area of the city, the Kingdom of Christ has a growing foothold in an area where other powers seemed once to reign supreme. Ronnie's story corroborates Cyril's experience in Nigeria and other parts of Africa, which prompted him to define religious conversion in Africa as "an encounter between two systems of salvation, resulting in a movement, on the part of the people, in the direction of power."[12]

This is not just confined to the so-called Two-Thirds World. It should not surprise us that as rationalism has eroded away in the more prosperous areas of the world, spiritually hungry individuals have begun looking to "the New Age" for health and healing, unaware that they are dealing with potentially lethal forces. We are starting to hear increasing numbers of stories about healings and miracles similar to those Ronnie Liew En Khiam sees regularly as Christ is invited into such situations. We expect this relative trickle to grow into a mighty flood.

Church Planting

Where there is a commitment to evangelism, there is an almost inevitable multiplication of congregations.   Conversely, when Christians lose their enthusiasm for evangelistic witness, church-planting grinds to a halt. Statistical evidence confirms that more outsiders are likely to come to faith within the context of brand new congregations, than through most older, more established parishes.

One of the most encouraging trends in the Episcopal Church in the USA in the last decade has been a renewed interest in planning and planting of new congregations. Despite significant population growth, continued migration to America, and massive population relocations within the country, the Episcopal Church had done little to encourage church-planting for at least 30 years. In 1991, almost as an afterthought, the General Convention committed the church to planting 1,000 new congregations before the year 2000. Although that target might be missed, an encouraging start has been made; 1995 saw the launch of a new voluntary agency to focus on church-planting and to assist church-planters. During its first year in existence, the North American Missionary Society made considerable progress working toward the establishing of new Episcopal churches in various parts of the USA.[13]

There has also been a renewed interest in church-planting in Britain, although new congregational development has often been hampered by parishes whose geographical boundaries are often jealously guarded by turf-conscious clergy. It is sad that a tired organizational structure, appropriate several centuries ago, now hinders new congregational development. Furthermore, instead of learning from the success of others, the Church of England seems to have been using an approach which is not the most effective.

"(New congregations) are attached by a runner either to the sending parish or the runner is attached to the church of the receiving parish. Rarely is it a completely new independent self-governing, self-sustaining and self-propagating plant established. As any good gardener will know, a new plant will only grow vigorously and mature fully if it is severed from the parent plant... Church of England planters seem not to have imbibed this fundamental point in the way the newer churches and some other denominations... have done."[14]

Despite this, new congregations are being born. The Church of England reports that church plants are accelerating. During the first three years of the Decade of Evangelism 102 new congregations came into being, but now they are looking at a new congregation being launched *every week* somewhere in England. Alas, churches are still dying: in the first three years of the Decade 84 congregations were "made redundant."[15]

Sadly, where new Anglican congregations have spilled over into "someone else's parish" and met with either a cold shoulder or outright opposition, it has been necessary for an unofficial non-geographical jurisdiction to provide oversight. The Federation of Independent Anglican Churches (FIAC) was formed in 1992, and while committed to the faith and order of the Anglican tradition, refuses to be bound by outmoded patterns. Its very existence is an indictment upon a church incapable of breaking out of "old wineskins."

Will the Church of England have to re-learn the painful lesson which the loss of Methodism two centuries ago should have taught it? This willingness to sacrifice opportunity for structural organizational orderliness sadly seems to be a besetting Anglican sin. If God does something new, rather than looking for ways to accommodate the new work and maximize its impact, we demand that it fit itself into what is there already, even if the existing framework is not particularly effective itself. We would probably be extremely alarmed if we knew how many good people and potentially exciting congregations have been lost because leaders have clung resolutely to a so-called "good church order."

Thankfully, church-planting in other parts of the world is not bound by the same historical strictures. When Tanzania became independent in the mid-1960s, the Diocese of Central Tanganyika covered two-thirds of this large East African country. Since that time the membership of the Church of the Province of Tanzania, in just this one diocese, has increased 20% per year. The result has been the division and sub-division of the mother diocese, until now there are eleven dioceses. This spectacular growth is illustrated by the remarkable progress made in a 24-month period in just one small geographical area. During that time several dozen congregations were established, and at time of writing they make up 13 new parishes. Tanzania is no isolated incident, as we have seen, with evangelistic efforts bearing extraordinary fruit in places as diverse as Nigeria and West Malaysia.

In the West it is unlikely we will see such thrilling statistics as quickly as we would like, but the potential illustrates how church-planting ought to be high on every agenda. We reiterate the truth stated earlier — newly-planted congregations are the ones most likely to reach out and present Christ to those who are spiritually hungry.

The Catechumenate

Where the Christian faith has been established for generations, there is a tendency to view baptism as the respectable rite of passage at birth, and confirmation as the rite of graduation out of the church at adolescence. Many a priest in the Western world has fought ferocious battles with angry parents when attempting to instigate a more realistic approach to confirmation and Christian formation. "I want to get my Eric (or Erica) 'done' before he (she) gets too old for church altogether, Rector," are words echoed a million times over around the world when the pastor has tried to explain that baptism and confirmation are about commitment. The faulty assumption on which these parents work is that all teenagers are going to drop out, and that the imposition of the bishop's hands upon their heads will somehow guarantee their future return.

We noted earlier that even when people make a personal commitment to Christ, there is a fearful falling away. It is obvious that a major contributing factor to young people departing in droves and new converts falling away, is a lack of nurture — we seek decisions, but we don't attempt to form disciples. Christian leaders also err in the direction of generosity when they look at their congregations, assuming people have a deeper grasp of the essentials of the faith than is true. What Christian researcher George Barna wrote about the North American scene is probably the case in many other parts of the world:

"We tend to think that everyone knows the basics... The research shows that while people may have some 'head knowledge' related to the Faith, they have insufficient context to comprehend what the beliefs have to do with day to day reality... We cannot assume that when we urge people to pray, they know what that means... Even on matters of knowledge, the research indicates that while people use concepts such as 'sin' and the 'Trinity' in polite conversation, they have little idea how those concepts fit into a deeper spiritual perspective."[16]

As the environment in which the churches live out their discipleship becomes increasingly hostile, there has been the slow realization that we need to return to an understanding of baptism as initiation into a missionary community, and that proper Christian formation requires more than a few childhood minutes each weekend in Sunday School. Beginning with the very young and going through to the very old, formation is a lifelong process. Liturgical revision has enabled Anglicans to accentuate these truths in their baptismal covenants, and in countries like the USA and New Zealand every effort is being made to transform liturgical form into pastoral and evangelistic reality. But it is a long term process, the fruits of which will take many years to see.[17]

A variety of programs, modeled on the ancient rites of the catechumenate, have sprung up. Implicit in these programs is the notion that formation and spiritual growth are not only for the unbaptized who are seeking after the faith, but also for those who are baptized but might be ignorant of it. Within this context, they are given every opportunity to respond afresh to the claims of Christ, or even to encounter the Lord at a personal level for the very first time.

At heart, the methodology of the catechumenate is simple. People are gathered together, allowed to inquire, and given the opportunity to ask questions so they might better understand the meaning and cost of Christian discipleship. Reflection upon Scripture is at its heart, and the whole process is understood as an opportunity to grasp the meaning of the journey of faith. Again and again where this has been tried, nominal Christians have found their baptismal faith ignited, and their own lives turned upside down.

Cyril Okorocha crossing the Equator
with Stephen Mungome to take the
Gospel to the rural areas of Uganda.

A Sunday service in Tonga, 1995.

Children in Tonga experience mission through schools.

Canon Dr. James Wong outside his main parish church,
Chapel of the Resurrection, Singapore.

Ministry with the deaf in Egypt, based at this
church center and school. The congregation poses
after morning service with the Bishop of Egypt,
the Rt. Rev. Ghais Malik.

This family in West Malaysia are converts from
Hinduism, and were all baptized in one day.

New church building in a parish in the Diocese on the Niger, East Nigeria. The sanctuary seats 5,000 people, and was built within two years (1992-94) in response to rapid growth.

In East Nigeria, women are the driving force behind the dynamic expansion and ministry of the church.

A small study guide, *Christian Growth, Maturity, and Discipleship,* designed originally for use in pre-worship Bible studies, has played a crucial part in the on-going renewal of the church in Nigeria.[18] One bishop has seen his diocese revolutionized by groups of Christians who have used this little book; he described it as "spiritual dynamite." An evangelistic crusade which drew crowds of more than 20,000 was held in the fields around his cathedral, and over 8,000 copies were used for follow-up. The Alpha Course, which we have already mentioned, is clearly doing something similar in parishes throughout Britain — and now into the rest of the world. The Anglican tradition has the learning, the tradition, and the liturgy. Set alight by the Holy Spirit, who knows how the fires of faith will rage?

In the Diocese of Milwaukee in the USA, the catechumenal program is known as *Journey In Faith.* Here is the testimony of one of the earlier participants in this ministry:

> The thing that struck me about *Journey In Faith,* when at last I understood it, was that it made perfect sense. What could be more central to our lives as Christians than examining, exploring, then putting into action our very faith? I marvel at its simplicity... Much to my surprise and relief, telling my story to another person was at once reassuring and liberating. I now view the faith story as a piece of 'standard equipment' for Episcopalians that we should have tucked away and ready at all times."[19]

Evangelism as a Process

What is distinctive about the approaches to evangelism we have outline above is that they rely to only a small extent on special evangelistic events. Everywhere in the world evangelism is increasingly being undertaken as a natural and on-going process in the life of the congregation. It is approached in a variety of ways, but will almost invariably grow out of the life of the Christian community, and be anchored in its day-by-day activities.

In Africa, for example, it is plain to see that making Christ known is normative, but the Western churches have a long way to go to recover this sense of urgency and priority. It is bound to change dioceses and parishes beyond recognition. We are called in our life together to reflect the values of the Gospel, proclaim the message, and seek those who are lost and bewildered. "The whole Church may need to be re-initiated, not in terms of rites or sacraments, but in terms of the reality of not just praying, but also living, the Lord's Prayer with its commitment to seek first the Kingdom of God. As Revd. John Cole, diocesan missioner for Lincoln diocese has put it: being more effectively evangelistic is not a matter of trying to learn new skills on the cheap but is a deeply costly matter of accepting God's gracious purposes and capacity in Christ to transform the whole of our lives."[20]

Heavenly Father,
you have called your Church to proclaim the Gospel in all lands:
help us in obedience to your call to participate actively in the
Christian mission in our own country and overseas,
and to commend the gospel of Christ
by what we are,
by what we say,
and by what we do for others,
to the glory of your name. Amen
(A Prayer of Canon Frank Colquhoun)[21]

What we have said:

■ Evangelistic churches are those that go out looking for people, rather than sitting and waiting to see who will cross the "stained glass barrier."

■ At the heart of evangelism is the believer's witness to the one who is seeking after faith.

■ Preaching both in churches and in public places is a strong element in the evangelistic tradition. But it requires imagination and creativity.

■ Cell groups which multiply provide a caring, safe environment in which seekers can explore the Christian faith and its implications.

■ In most parts of the world, the power of God displayed in signs, wonders, and healings that tends to draw people to Jesus Christ.

■ The continual commitment to planting new congregations is fundamental to healthy Christian growth.

■ The recovery of the ancient tradition of the catechumenate has enabled nominal Christians as well as outsiders to explore the meaning of the faith and apply it to their lives.

Thinking it over:

■ Read John 4.1-38. Examine the way Jesus drew the woman into conversation and led her into a personal encounter with the Messiah, himself. What is he trying to teach us in the churches today about personal evangelism and Christian witness?

■ Is there a "stained glass barrier" between the people inside your congregation and the world outside? If so, how do you think you can go about removing it?

■ Talk about the place of signs, wonders, miracles, and healings in the ministry of evangelism. Do you think this is something for all Christians, or just for those who live in countries where such a diverse spiritual world is understood?

■ Talk together about the ways your parish can reach out to those in the area who are merely nominal Christians.

CHAPTER EIGHT
Renewal and Evangelism

"The first need in evangelism is for a strengthening and a quickening of spiritual life within the Church."
— CHURCH OF ENGLAND REPORT,
"TOWARDS THE CONVERSION OF ENGLAND," PUBLISHED IN 1944

What is Renewal?

Ask any dozen Christians to define the term "renewal" and you are likely to get a dozen different answers. In some quarters, even mention of the word will raise hackles and set teeth on edge. In other settings "renewal" is not only good, but many Christians think it is the only hope for the churches.

Part of the problem is the tendency to confuse the externals with the reality. Renewal is the process whereby the Holy Spirit prepares the church for mission, enabling Christians to participate with confidence and vigor in the *Missio Dei*. That it is often accompanied by exuberant styles of worship and other phenomena which make some feel uncomfortable is immaterial — these are merely the "packaging." When God renews the church, new potency is added to the whole rich stream of the Christian heritage found in the creeds. Within the Anglican world today a "convergence of the saints" is taking place as various styles of creedal Christianity and renewal jostle, merge, feed, and enrich one another.[1] Charismatics, often viewed as noisy and unreflective people, are discovering the secret of silence, guided retreats in a monastic setting, and are exploring various social expressions of the Gospel. Anglo-Catholics, on the other hand, are being loosened up as their tradition is cross-fertilized with other approaches.

Bishop David Pytches believes the renewing work of the Holy Spirit "generates new energy, fresh motivation and the spontaneous expansion of the church,"[2] while Alister McGrath suggests that "renewal may well mean a painful process of self-examination, in which many cherished ideas and approaches of the past are set to one side as redundant and unhelpful."[3] Perhaps it is fair to say that reflection follows in the wake of the initiatives of God, the Holy Spirit guiding the Body of Christ forward as it seeks to clean house, readying itself for the mission to which it has been called and commissioned. Renewal sets the scene for mission.

Churches of the Anglican Communion throughout the world have experienced renewal in varying degrees and forms during the last thirty years. As the fresh breath of renewal has progressed from stumbling infancy to adulthood, it has been altering and reshaping us, especially the way we worship. When renewal is genuine, it is accompanied by qualities and characteristics which marked the life of the early church. As it seeps more deeply into the life of the Christian community it alters priorities and ethics, and brings these into closer conformity with the New Testament.

Those who have experienced afresh the power of God through the Holy Spirit, whether as a still small voice or as a mighty rushing wind, are the ones most likely to be burdened by the need for ethical and social change. Perhaps one of the tragedies of renewal movements has been the manner in which folks have often allowed themselves to be diverted into selfish other-worldliness and "gifts mania," while the power of such a divine invasion for personal and social transformation, which issues in selfless service of God and society, is lost. True revival transforms sinners into saints, and self-seeking egotists into selfless servants of God and God's people in the world.

Revival in Nigeria

The Nigerian church is a good example of God's renewing work. We focus on Nigeria not because it is the only place in the world where something like this has happened, but because Cyril Okorocha is Nigerian, and played a meaningful part in these exciting movements of God's Spirit.

Prior to the crisis in the mid-1960s which led to the Nigerian civil war, the churches had grown fat and comfortable, unable to recognize — let alone challenge — the excesses of Nigeria's political leaders. These injustices triggered social discontent which led to a military coup, which in turn resulted in hideous pogroms directed against the predominantly Christian Igbo, by Hansa-Fulani people, who are largely Muslim. When the mainly Christian peoples of eastern Nigeria seceded from the federation, war broke out.

With war raging all around them, young people, mostly high school students, began meeting for Bible study and prayer at the local headquarters of the Scripture Union in Umuahia. By then Umuahia was the unofficial capital of Biafra, as Enugu, their major city, had already been overrun by federal forces. Schools and colleges had been closed, and these young people roamed the streets because there was not much else to do. These gatherings became a meeting place for students and young people too young or unwilling to enroll in the armed forces.

Bill Roberts, an Englishman, led them, having chosen to share the fate of the Biafran people, rather than flee with other ex-patriates who had long since left the secessionist region. Cyril Okorocha, a high schooler who had committed his life to Christ, was enlisted by Bill to be one of his assistants. At first, the meetings were held once a week, but quickly became daily — and there in the heart of a war zone, the Spirit of God broke in upon these students gathered for Bible study and prayer in an unpremeditated, unplanned way. It was like a page from the Acts of the Apostles! This started a renewal which would eventually spread to the rest of Nigeria — even to other parts of West Africa.

As the population fled from the advancing war, this revival was carried by the young people from village to village. These vast dislocations of population accelerated this spread of the Gospel. When hostilities ended with the demise of Biafra in January 1970, virtually every village and refugee camp had become a center of renewal. Spiritual euphoria did not last for too long. Those who experienced renewal started picking up the reins of their lives, returning to university or to work. As people settled back into a normal existence in the following twelve months, tension quickly developed between the leaders of the mainline churches, and the young revivalists whose interdenominational approach to the faith, charismatic style of preaching, and emphasis upon personal holiness they found extremely threatening.[4]

Many of the young were either expelled or frozen out of the mainline churches, leaving to set up their own movements. Some remained, or more accurately, they refused to be pushed out! Cyril was one who refused to budge. In the months following the war's end, with a recently converted graduate of the University of Ibadan named Mike, he worked with the Scripture Union to take the revival into colleges and schools in the West and Midwestern Nigeria, and some parts of the mostly Muslim North. Today Mike is a minister of the Methodist Church.

One of those frozen out of the Anglican Church was Chinedu Nebo, someone we have already met in this book. That Dr. Nebo is today a priest is evidence of the changed spiritual climate in the Anglican Church.[5] God's Spirit is once more on the move in Nigeria as those influenced by the earlier revival reach positions of influence in the Anglican church. There is once more a fresh thirst for God; as Chinedu Nebo puts it, "The time has passed for dead men preaching dead sermons to dead congregations at a dead time on Sunday mornings." The older leaders have got the message: either accept this vibrancy of faith or your churches will empty out!

Those young leaders are maturing, and the Evangelical Fellowship of the Anglican Communion (EFAC), to which many of them belong, is maturing with them. EFAC in Nigeria is a forum in which ideas and dreams can be explored, and the setting from which many fresh initiatives have emerged. Some suggest that what the Church Mission Society (CMS) was to the Nigerian church in the pioneer missionary years of the mid-nineteenth century, and what Scripture Union was to the church during the early years of the revival, EFAC has become today.[6]

Remarkably, EFAC in Nigeria is 90% lay in its membership, with huge numbers of young women and men willing to learn the real cost of discipleship. They have discovered the joy which accompanies the sacrificial spending of time, treasure, talents, and energy in the service of Jesus Christ and the spread of his Kingdom. Whenever genuine renewal takes place, the level of commitment rises. Perhaps the greatest lesson to be learned from the impact EFAC is making in Nigeria, is that whenever the laity are empowered by the Holy Spirit for ministry, the whole church bursts into life. The church belongs to the laity. The clergy must discover what it is to be enablers — using their skills to build up and empower "ordinary" Christians to exercise their God-given ministry wherever they happen to be.

Further Lessons from Nigeria

While we are not suggesting that the Nigerian church is perfect, by any means, it is a clear example of what God does when his Spirit invades the lives of his people in renewal and the revival of personal holiness. Empowerment for mission grows out of a fresh confidence in the Gospel, as well as a new but on-going experience of repentance and forgiveness, including the reconciliation of those who are at odds with one another. When a renewed church commits itself to evangelism, not only does it become sacrificial, it also becomes generous and bountiful.

What's more, the way it handles its resources will be totally transformed. If mission is the cutting edge of the church's ministry, then those who have been renewed quickly realize that this is where good stewards invest their spiritual and material wealth. We ought not kid ourselves that we can buy our way into the Kingdom of God: but when writing to the Corinthians, Paul made it clear that giving for mission is one of the best barometers for measuring the level of our spirituality and sense of indebtedness to the one who gave himself for us.[7]

There are still those in the Nigerian church who are happy to sit and warm a pew on Sunday mornings, or who feel threatened by the new life surging around them. But things are changing for the better because a critical mass of women and men have made their lives totally available for God to use in mission. The result is that parishes are being revived, churches are being planted, dioceses are multiplying, and fresh ground is being broken for Christ's Kingdom.

One of the most important things that happened at the G-CODE 2000 gathering might have been the realization by the churches in West Africa that God is calling Anglicans there to form their own missionary sending agency. Could it be that in years to come, through this agency (or something like it), increasing numbers of committed Nigerians will not only be reaching out cross-culturally, but will be playing a leading role as Anglicans play their part tackling the challenge of World A? Might we not also see their vibrancy of faith bringing renewal to the old, tired Western churches as they face up to the difficult challenge posed by the need to re-evangelize their countries? We certainly hope so!

Into All the World With SOMA

Sharing Of Ministries Abroad (SOMA), brainchild of the English charismatic leader, Michael Harper, has played a growing and valuable role in the worldwide mission of the Anglican Communion, through lives profoundly changed by the renewing work of the Holy Spirit. SOMA is now getting off the ground in Southern Africa, but it is already well-established in the United Kingdom, Ireland, Canada, Australia, New Zealand, and the USA. The ministry of SOMA illustrates how a fresh vision for the work of God around the world can be imparted to those who have experienced renewal — and who as a result want to dedicate their lives to Christian service.

Each year, SOMA enables scores of Christians to spend up to a month involved in a short-term mission somewhere in the world where their spiritual gifts or other skills can be used. Usually these missioners go at their own expense, or with the help of their parishes. SOMA teams are not mavericks, but only visit dioceses from which they receive an invitation from the bishop. They most often go to conduct leadership conferences for clergy and laity and renewal missions. Most of those who participate in SOMA's ministry return transformed — and with a new vision of God at work in the world.

SOMA never imposes itself or its vision on the dioceses they visit; rather they respond to the particular needs or concerns a diocese may have. Missioners from SOMA go as servants to the servants of God in these various places. Their goal is to equip believers for ministry in such a way that the mission of the church can advance when the missioners from abroad have gone.

The needs churches have are varied, as are the ways Western Christians can help. Take the Spanish-speaking Caribbean country of the Dominican Republic, for example. Not long ago, Bishop Bill Frey, retired Dean of Trinity Episcopal School for Ministry, former Bishop of Colorado, and himself once a missionary in Latin America, was invited with his wife, Barbara, to conduct a week-long crusade-style evangelistic campaign in the diocese. The challenge facing the diocese was the need to train people to be counselors to those who might make a personal commitment to Jesus Christ as a result of the bishop's preaching. In this instance, SOMA sent a team to the Caribbean and, during the week leading up to the campaign, they undertook in-depth training of counselors, and prayed for the success of the mission.

The challenge facing the Chapel of St. Francis, on the campus of Makerere University, Kampala, Uganda, was rather different. Given the changing cultural environment in East Africa, the university chaplain, Benoni Mugarura-Mutana, was increasingly frustrated by the way the traditional Ugandan approach to Anglican worship "turned off" the college students among whom he ministers. Ben believes, quite rightly, that living, relevant worship is vital if the young are to have the opportunity for a genuine encounter with Jesus Christ. Churchy "saying of prayers" will never cut any ice. He was also worried that the model to which many Ugandan students seemed to be attracted was the entertainment-oriented approach of the media evangelists buying time on television. The same style dominates in a rash of largely non-denominational churches which have sprouted all over the country.

The SOMA teams that went to Uganda in 1994 and 1995 were commissioned to work with Ben Mugarura-Mutana and his congregation as they explored ways in which spiritual renewal, contemporary music, and the richness of the liturgy can be mingled within the Ugandan context. The teams were led by Alison Barfoot, an American Episcopal priest and trained musician. This was not an attempt to impose a western style upon those who attended the conferences and seminars, but an effort to allow principles to surface which might then be adapted to the prevailing culture in Ugandan congregations. One of Alison's most startling realizations was the way so many young Ugandans aspire to be like Americans! Despite an obvious renewed interest in indigenous cultures in Africa, the young are fairly and squarely being absorbed by the rapidly emerging global youth culture.

These SOMA teams to Uganda not only taught, but committed themselves to training local Christians in this ministry, integrating members of the University Chapel into their company, and training them to lead similar seminars in various provincial centers in different parts of the country. The result is a cadre of men and women who are teaching this fresh approach to worship all over the country. The long-term goal is to help Uganda's young recognize that the service and worship of God can be lively, and that one does not have to be either English or live in yesteryear to be an Anglican Christian!

Renewal for Service

These are just two examples of the power of renewal in evangelism and mission which we have chosen from many more we have before us. They clearly illustrate that when God renews the church it benefits the people who respond to God's fresh blessing and go out in service, as well as their churches back at home. Edwina Thomas, Executive Director of SOMA-USA, believes that, while SOMA's work around the world has a profound and positive influence on the church to which teams are sent, it has far more impact on congregation, doing the sending.

SOMA encourages parishes to take sending seriously. It is relatively easy to draw up a team of volunteers, but these may not be the right people with the right gifts. Instead, congregations are challenged to identify those gifted for the task, and then to commission them as short-term representatives of that community, charging them to bring back the story of what has happened. As it prays for the mission, then hears the results, the home parish is almost always blessed and is then eager to take the next step into deeper obedience to the Great Commission. The Holy Spirit seems to be drawing the churches' attention to the paradoxical truth that not only is there blessing in giving and going, but from that experience comes a deepened consciousness of our own needs — and the way God meets them.

As we talked with Edwina, she rattled off the names of parishes whose whole approach to the evangelistic task has been transformed by sending out SOMA mission teams. Not only have the experiences and reports back enabled them to see the world through different eyes, but their whole approach to ministry at home is challenged and upgraded. When a parishioner goes out to share something of the Gospel in another place and comes back rejoicing and telling stories of conversions and miracles, the congregation discovers how much they are partners with Christ through the ministry of intercessory prayer. Here, at the grass roots level, churches are learning what partnership in mission is all about, and how we are interdependent on one another.

Renewal Builds Up Lighthouse Congregations

From time to time God does something extraordinary in a particular congregation which makes it a focal point toward which other Christians look, and from whom they then learn. These parishes are, in a way, like lighthouses, guiding other Christians to find a new approach to ministry. Such congregations are to be found all over the world.

Clearly, the Chapel of St. Francis at Makerere University in Kampala is one, while another is Holy Trinity Church on London's Brompton Road. We have already talked about the Alpha Course they have developed, a program that lays firm foundations for effective Christian living and witness, which they are now sharing with all the world. The principles and teachings of the Alpha Course have been popularized with easy-to-read books and pamphlets, videos and audio tapes. As we write, Alpha is being used in more than 750 churches in England — as well as in thirteen other countries. By the time this book is published, we suspect Alpha will be in many more places. Alpha provides setting in which outsiders — as well as insiders who aren't so sure of the fundamentals — can get to grips with the basics of the faith without being set upon or made to feel stupid.

In the 1970s and 1980s, St. Paul's Church, Darien, Connecticut, and Truro Episcopal Church, Fairfax, Virginia, became important centers in the American church. Having experienced explosive growth both in numbers and in spiritual depth, these parishes were able to share what had been happening with lay and ordained leaders from other congregations all over North America. In the 1990s other parishes, like All Saints', Pawleys Island, South Carolina, have been raised up to fulfill a similar role.

Each of these congregations, together with others in various renewal traditions, have done an extraordinary job teaching their people the fundamentals of financial stewardship. This in turn has led to growing budgets from which a significant proportion is set aside for mission and outreach. Parishes like Truro Church, and dioceses like Alabama, aim toward giving away 50% of their total income. Gifts like these lubricate the mission of the church in many corners of the world, where opportunities otherwise die on the vine for want of funds. The gift from the people in Fairfax, Virginia, was crucial in the launch of the Diocese of the Rift Valley in Tanzania, for example.

Perhaps the greatest blind spot in the patterns of giving among many of these congregations and dioceses, is to reach out with the Gospel to the least evangelized. This seems to reflect a tendency in renewal circles to put an immediate experience of God before any long-range strategy to reach the world with the Gospel message. We hope that in the years to come we will see a greater willingness on the part of all Christians — but especially those who can make a significant difference — to give support to the proclamation of the Good News in exciting and innovative ways in those places where the message of salvation has yet to be heard and responded to.

Whole books have been written on the topic of renewal, so it is impossible for us to do it justice in a handful of pages. However, it is incumbent on all of us continually to pray and work toward the renewal of the church. As we do so, God will do wondrous things in a whole variety of ways, leaving us both amazed and awestruck. The Church in Nigeria stands before us as an example of what God can do to a whole province of a worldwide communion, if the person of the Holy Spirit is allowed to have his way. The Church in Laodicea stands as a warning to us. Christ told that congregation in the Revelation to St. John, "I know your works: you are neither cold nor hot... Would that you were cold or hot! So, because you are lukewarm, and neither cold nor hot, I will spew you out of my mouth."[8] We prefer the embarrassing extremism which sometimes accompanies renewal, to Christianity which is vacuous, or which already has one foot in the grave!

◆◆◆◆◆

Lord God, in Christ you make all things new.
Grant to your Church a new vision of your glory,
a new experience of your power, a new consecration to your service;
that through the witness of a renewed and dedicated people
your work may be revived and your kingdom extended among us,
for the honor of your name. Amen

(A Prayer of Canon Frank Colquhoun)[9]

What we have said:

■ The Holy Spirit renews the church so that it might be effective in its mission.

■ Genuine renewal should lead to intense and painful self-examination.

■ Renewal restores confidence in the Scriptures, drawing persons closer to God for the purpose of Christian service.

■ Worship, renewal, and evangelism are closely related.

■ Parishes which get involved in mission ministries away from home experience new infusions of life into the work they do on their own doorsteps.

■ God raises up parishes to act as beacons and lighthouses.

■ Renewal has financial stewardship implications.

Thinking it over:

■ Is Bishop Pytches right when he suggests that renewal leads to the spontaneous expansion of the church? What might prevent this?

■ Why is there a relationship between a renewed experience of the Gospel, repentance, forgiveness, and a willingness to engage in evangelism?

■ Is the Prayer Book liturgy a help or a hindrance in renewed worship?

■ What are the financial implications for us as we express our commitment to Christ?

■ Read Revelation 3.14-22. What do Christ's words to the church in Laodicea have to say to us as we seek to witness for him today?

CHAPTER NINE
What Does a Growing Church Look Like?

"Every worshipping community should be encouraged to see the whole picture of its apostolic calling and become committed to it."
— ARCHBISHOP BRIAN DAVIS OF NEW ZEALAND[1]

One of us is African, the other European. Cyril Okorocha, the African, now lives in Europe, while Richard Kew, the European, has lived and worked in North America for the last 20 years. Cyril is the Director of Evangelism and Mission for the worldwide Anglican Communion, an evangelist, mission scholar, pastor, and theologian. Richard, for his part, has been involved in the launch and development of a number of Episcopal mission agencies during his time in the USA, and is also a writer, speaker, and pastor. Both of us are priests. From our two unusual and very different vantage points we have seen a great deal of world Christianity as both participants and as "involved observers."

None of the churches we have visited are perfect; indeed, all of them have their share of ugly blemishes. Nor are any two churches exactly alike. Yet despite shortcomings and differences there seem to be characteristics which set apart congregations, dioceses, and national churches which are growing, and have a wholehearted commitment to mission. While the Holy Spirit has never created ecclesiastical clones, we have recognized that certain qualities are constants in most settings.

1. Evangelistic, Growing Churches are Praying Churches:

There is a tendency to fast forward when we see a heading like this one. It seems such a boring truism. We have heard it a thousand times, "Prayer changes things..." "Prayer is the answer..." or "We are praying for you..." Why waste time being bombarded by it again? The answer is simple: because it is something about which we *need* continual reminding. We tend to get so caught up in activities, strategies, and techniques, that we overlook the organic link between our relationship with God and its impact upon our ministry.

Prayer begins in the heart of God, as does the yearning that all persons everywhere should come to know the Almighty not only as Creator, but also as Redeemer and Lord. If these two facets of Christian discipleship have the same starting point, then they are clearly going to feed upon and nurture one another. Lady Gill Brentford, speaking at G-CODE 2000 of the way she and her husband, an active and influential member of the House of Lords, live out their faith in the British Parliament, stated with great clarity and conviction, "Prayer is where it all starts."[2]

Churches that are effective in evangelism pray, and pray fervently. Their prayers are a delightful mixture of adoration, repentance, and intercession, and as they reach ever more deeply into the mind of God, so God's passion for the world grows in their hearts. As Gill Brentford told of evangelism around Parliament, it was obvious that the Christians who work in this place where temporal power is all important, have a deep understanding of the resources of spiritual power available to them.

This is not just a discovery of those involved with the Mother of Parliaments; it is a conviction they share with Christians everywhere. Often, over the centuries, it has been forgotten and then rediscovered with great excitement that "more things are wrought by prayer than the world dreams of." Whenever revival has broken out, at its roots have been insignificant people, a group of youngsters, for example, who have been praying. Both the New Testament and the missionary history of the church confirm this.

The apostles were at prayer on the day of Pentecost when the Holy Spirit burst in upon them. Again, when they faced severe persecution from the Jerusalem establishment, and had no one to whom they could appeal, they gave themselves to prayer.[3]

It is no accident that things started happening when Count Nicholas Von Zinzendorf set aside his home, Herrnhut, in Bohemia, for the ministry of prayer. From 1737, Herrnhut was maintained for more than a hundred years by Christians who believed in the power of prayer. It was the power released through the prayer of this small group which fueled the spread of Moravian missions, coinciding with the conversions to Christ of John Wesley and George Whitefield, the Great Awakening of the 18th Century, the rise of Methodism, and the early blossoming of the modern missionary movement. When saints sink to their knees in prayer, extraordinary things are bound to happen! That little prayer band of Moravians remain a model for us today.

During the last few years, the example of Zinzendorf and the Hundred Year Prayer Meeting has been followed by increasing numbers. Great concerts of prayer for the world are now in full swing. There are 6,000-7,000 Roman Catholic religious communities praying continually for global evangelization, while several concerts of prayer link a variety of Protestant groups. The special ministry of intercession is making a spectacular come-back, and we are finding women and men in churches everywhere whom God has gifted in this area.

The G-CODE 2000 conference, which we believe is beginning to have a profound impact around the world, was rooted in prayer, and borne along on the wings of creative worship. At all times during the gathering a team of intercessors were at work, and one morning Archbishop Carey joined them for an hour. What is true on a national and international level needs also to be true in the life of the local churches. There is no reason at all why parishes, deaneries, archdeaconaries and dioceses should not be offering a steady flow of prayers for God's guidance and blessing on their mission.

The Korean Pentecostal pastor, David Yonggi Choi, whose Full Gospel congregation in Seoul now numbers more than 800,000 members, believes his church is tangible evidence of the power of prayer. He is also convinced that the prayers of his congregation — in fellowship with others around South Korea — played a significant role in the dislodging dictatorship in their country, and have held communism at bay. Choi's church is a praying church and a missionary church — these two belonging together. They pray fervently for the mission of the church, in their thousands of home groups during the week and at seven services every Sunday. This congregation alone is served by over 700 pastors, and supports 700 missionaries ministering around the world!

Replicating such congregations might be difficult, but emulating them in the ministry of prayer and intercession is something for which we should be striving. If there is one thing which is a constant in evangelistic congregations around the world, it is their realization that prayer must be at the heart of their mission.

2. Growing Churches Listen to God:

There is nothing worse than one-sided conversations. Standard fare in any television sitcom is the gossiping woman from whom everyone wants to escape, or the boorish male who will trap you for hours, forcing upon you his "stories." Prayer without listening to God's response is hardly prayer at all; it is more like one of these one-sided conversations. Churches that know how to pray with fervor have also usually learned to listen. God frequently speaks, as he tends to move, in mysterious ways, which means we should be attentive to what he is saying.

A few years ago, the Church in Nigeria recognized that it had an enormous mission field within the boundaries of its own country, among predominantly Muslim peoples in the north. It was an issue they talked about, and prayed over. The message seemed to come from God that if they waited until they felt ready to reach into this area, they would never get on with the job. Today there are eight missionary dioceses which are proclaiming with courage and sensitivity Christ crucified and risen in that difficult corner of the African vineyard — and God is blessing this venture of faith.

For many years now it has been a practice in Santiago, Chile, for the parishes in the city to hold an all night prayer vigil once a month. Beginning from almost nothing in Chile's cities 25 years ago, the diocese is today nearly 100 congregations strong, and has plans for aggressive expansion. Clearly those times when the church gives itself to knowing God's will through prayer, are times that have helped fuel this encouraging growth of witness and ministry.

God's answers to prayer may come in many forms: through a convergence of circumstances, a growing sense that a meditated course of action is right, or (and this is less probable), through a prophetic word or a vision. However God speaks, it is the responsibility of the churches to hear and respond.   William Temple, the great Archbishop of Canterbury during the Second World War, remarked that coincidences stop happening when Christians stop praying. Someone, building on Archbishop Temple's idea, says that there are no co-incidences for Christians, just *God-incidences!*

3. A Growing Church is a Worshipping Church:

This looks like another one of those bothersome truisms, as it is normally assumed that worship is at the heart of any congregation's life — it is certainly the most visible activity in which it involves itself. Yet, just as there is a great difference between praying and "saying our prayers," there is a qualitative difference between genuine worship and church attendance with rote repetition of the liturgy. A generation ago it was suggested that traditional Anglican worship is more like "a stately masked ball," than anything else. Such worship, if it appealed to any of the senses, was most likely to touch not much more than the intellect — if that! Dead worship is not much of a calling card for a living faith.

Things are changing. Almost everywhere today Anglican worship is a rich interweaving of languages, styles of music, bodily movements, and heartfelt praise. The African churches are working hard to find a synthesis of their own heritage with the historic, liturgical tradition of the church, while many Western churches have experienced a significant "loosening up." Latin Americans, Asians, and Arab Christians, among so many others,[4] are attempting to express themselves in worship that is rich, meaningful, and focused on the grandeur of God, while at the same time relevant to their own environment.

Worship that is creative and genuine issues from the depths of our being. It not only refreshes Christians, but also attracts newcomers. Worship at the G-CODE gathering was a sumptuous tapestry of Anglican styles. Led by Ugandan, John Sentamu,[5] and the Uganda Anglican Youth Choir, this intricate blend of music styles and liturgies from around the world was captivating. In wondrous ways God was in our midst! This often happens when worship is inspired by the Holy Spirit, anchored in believing prayer, and objectified in mission.

As with other Christian traditions, Anglicans have been rediscovering the centrality of the Eucharist, recognizing that the powerful symbols of bread broken and wine poured out can have a profound impact upon those searching for the Kingdom. Yet in North Carolina at the G-CODE conference, Raymond Fung, the Baptist from Hong Kong, wondered if Anglicans had not gone overboard on the Eucharist. He pointed out that there is "far too much concern about starting the evangelistic journey at the eucharistic table, and too little concern about evangelism ending up in the market place." In short, is sacramental worship seeker-sensitive? Perhaps one of the big issues in coming years is whether worship that is so strongly sacramental is a help or hindrance evangelistically.

Andrew Knock and Dan Onwukwe, who wrote the Bible study handbook for G-CODE, disagree with Dr. Fung. They argue that the eucharistic table is both a celebration and an *invitation*. The Eucharist, symbolizing Christ's death and resurrection, is at the same time a celebration of the conquest of sin and the kingdom of darkness, and an invitation to new life in the new community of Light. This looks like the beginning of a very fruitful debate, as we seek to integrate both worship and mission — let us pursue it with vigor!

Benoni Mugarurra-Mutana, Chaplain of Makerere University in Uganda, has given considerable thought to the sort of worship that enables people to experience the presence of God. Over breakfast one dank mountain morning, he shared his passion. Working as he does among the young, he is troubled when he sees them going off to enthusiastic, but often misguided, neo-pentecostal churches where many tend to get hurt. "Meanwhile," he says sadly, shaking his head, "we die with the 1662 Prayer Book." The traditional approach to worship is too cultic, he argues, and totally detached from the realities of daily life in modern Uganda.

He talked with affection about Thomas Cranmer, the Archbishop of Canterbury during the Church of England's separation from Rome, and explained how the renewed liturgical tradition Cranmer created freed Reformation Christians, enabling them to worship God in both spirit and in truth. He sees the martyred archbishop as a model, asking, "My prayer is: Lord, how can we do it in these times?"

His congregation, the University Chapel of St. Francis, is exploring the richness of our worshipping tradition, from the charismatic through to the more formal. It must be doing something right. People like Helen Wangusa and her family are driving 30 or 40 minutes into Kampala to be there on Sundays, rather than staying closer to home and groaning over a boring Anglo-Saxon liturgy in a Bugandan village![6] Sitting beside her pastor at breakfast, she endorsed all he was saying, adding how meaningful worship at St. Francis's is to her impressionable and growing children. Helen's yearning is universal — and testimony the church needs to take very seriously.[7]

Ben concluded our conversation by saying, "At worship, we should experience the coming down of God among his people. He indwells us, walks among us — that has to be very evangelistic." Gulping down a final mouthful of coffee, this visionary Christian leader prepared to leave for a weekend preaching mission in Virginia. He is right — it is imperative that we discover how to worship in a way that is relevant, has a magnetic attraction, yet retains its richness.

There are many parts of the world where the very idea of an outsider making a casual visit to a church is highly unlikely. In these instances, to draw people in and give them the opportunity to consider the claims of Christ, our "worship" needs to be creative and our liturgy more imaginative — while remaining recognizably Christian.

The parish of St. Peters, Hextable, in Kent, England, is a place where limited resources are not preventing them from experimenting with outreach events. Targeting the 18-45 year olds, they have begun a series of Seeker Events which use video, photography, dance, music, and drama to explore the relevance of the Gospel to a particular contemporary theme. This illustrates the place of imagination, with occasional special events merging worship, entertainment, and apologetics. If we are to reach those who are alienated from or totally ignorant of the Christian faith, then creativity must be the order of the day.

The people of St. Peter's think that as these events develop, they have potential for reaching the unchurched, especially younger people. However, from the outset they realized that visitors are not going to come "cold." They need an invitation from a friend or neighbor just to get them over the threshold. Making such invitations is something that most parishioners should have no trouble doing.

4. *Growing Churches have Visionary Leadership:*

The prime pattern for Christian leadership must be Jesus, who divested himself of his own power and invested it in his followers, turning them from virtual nobodies into agents of global transformation. It is therefore interesting that in the last few years, management gurus have spent inordinate amounts of time studying the nature of leadership, because changing times like these require those at the helm who can not only lead, but also possess the vision to steer in the right direction.

The predominant leadership style in the Western churches today is managerial, which means they are led by organizers whose skills are most effective in stable times. In a more chaotic era, we need leaders who can see beyond the horizon, then communicate their vision with passion and develop new, transforming ways of doing things. A visionary leader does more than dream of what might happen, but has the capacity to translate those dreams into a workable plan, and then the courage to carry it out. It is vital that we call forth those gifted as transformers, then set them free to get on with the job.[8]

> "Vision is spawned by faith, sustained by hope, sparked by imagination and strengthened by enthusiasm. It is greater than sight, deeper than a dream, broader than an idea. Vision encompasses vast vistas outside the realm of the predictable, the safe, the expected."[9]

Vision springs from the inspiration of God, but is nurtured in human hearts. One of the more visionary parish priests in the 1970s was Terry Fullam, then Rector of St. Paul's, Darien, Connecticut, USA. Speaking of visionary leadership at that time, he said,

> "Vision is the product of God working in us. He creates the vision and we receive it; it becomes a rallying point, a goal toward which we move as his people... Vision arises out of our burden to know the will of God... Vision is something that elicits a response from us, that calls us forth. Goals, on the other hand are things we project... If I am to be part of the Body of Christ, it is not really a matter of 'Where do I want to go?' - but rather, 'Where does he want to take me?'"[10]

At G-CODE 2000 it was clear from the outset that there is a qualitative difference in African leadership, as well as that of many

Two-Thirds World churches, when compared to the older, more established churches. The manner in which reports were given, whether they came from Nigeria, Uganda, or East Asia, displayed an assurance of faith, and it was clear that these churches had a pretty good idea where God might take them in the future. Put simply, they were visionary.

Growing churches are led by vision bearers rather than problem solvers. The visionaries in North Carolina were involved in a cross-section of ministries, and were a variety of personality types, but when they started talking, there was a confidence and boldness which demonstrated that they knew what they were doing. Rennis Ponniah, a priest from Singapore, exclaimed, "The power of God drives our convictions." It would be wrong to suggest that only the burgeoning churches of the global South have visionary leaders. There are visionaries in the North, too, but amidst the confusion and within the context of churches that are often far from healthy, vision bearers get overlooked, labeled as troublemakers, or perhaps ignored altogether.

Churches that move forward in evangelism and mission are those whose leadership is courageous and always preparing for the future. These leaders are able to communicate the vision, yet are so sensitive to their followers that they confidently carry the majority with them. Where the church lacks such leadership, could it not be that God is prompting us to look prayerfully for effective ways of raising up a new breed of visionary standard bearers?

Could it be that there is a message here for those who select men and women for ordination and other leadership roles? Seminaries, theological colleges, and Bible schools that are training the next generation need to be asking some fundamental questions of themselves. Are yesterday's methods going to raise up and deploy imaginative visionaries, whose churches are moving forward in the power of the Spirit? There is a great deal of hard thinking and praying that needs to be done.

5. A Growing Church is an Equipped and Equipping Church:

Effective congregations take seriously the concept that every member of the Body of Christ is called to be a minister. It ought to be obvious to everyone who has eyes to see, that there isn't a member of the clergy alive today who is a compendium of all the gifts for ministry God has poured out!

The total mobilization of the People of God, marrying the evangelistic and the pastoral, is vital if the church is to move forward. When the first disciples found their way from Jerusalem to Antioch, it was not ordained clergy who "gossiped the gospel" all the way there, but ordinary "lay" men and women enthused by a knowledge of Jesus Christ which had transformed their lives. One of the characteristics Rennis Ponniah of Singapore believes typifies the church in Southeast Asia is its aim for the total mobilization of all its membership. In Singapore, cell groups are the basic substructure of every parish, and these have been settings in which total ministry is able to take place.

Since the Decade of Evangelism was launched, Michael Howard has been Adviser in Evangelism in the Diocese of Rochester, UK. By trial and error, Canon Howard has developed a program which trains lay evangelists. Michael believes that ordinary Christians are unlikely even to attempt to witness to their faith until they are, as it were, "given permission" to do so. Evangelism is incarnational and, continuing the analogy, they receive permission when they see folk like themselves living out what it means to be an evangelist in their daily life. The goal in Rochester is to enable people with evangelistic gifts to use them, and then to support these trained lay evangelists as they encourage others to witness for Christ.

A growing team of evangelists has been trained and commissioned, now "the challenge is to encourage clergy to use them to the full."[11] In the Church of England, as elsewhere, selection for ordination seems to favor the introverted rather than extroverts, and is biased toward those with pastoral rather than evangelistic instincts. "The result is that evangelism in the parishes is being blocked by clergy, who either do not have the gifts or the right people — or, if they have, are not willing to work collaboratively with them and develop lay ministry teams, which include evangelists. The training of evangelists is, therefore, highlighting another problem of ministry further down the line: how to help clergy to work in ministry teams and not be lone rangers."[12]

So we are back at training and selecting clergy again. Perhaps the greatest challenge before the churches and their seminaries, especially in those deep-rooted historic churches like our own, which have a highly developed theology of ordained ministry, is how to create clergy who cannot only handle an activated, evangelistic laity, but who also relish it! Given the nature of congregational dynamics, where the priest insists on being the "cork in the bottle," opportunities to turn a parish into a strong pastoral and evangelistic unit are going to be stymied.

6. Growing Churches Give Particular Attention to the Ministry of Women and Ministry Among Youth:

Reports from the growing churches in the global South given at the G-CODE gathering were unanimous in their praise of the work done by women all over the world. In Nigeria, Uganda, and Kenya, for instance, the Mothers' Union has for decades been a powerful instrument for evangelism, especially the evangelization of families, and for the healing of broken lives and troubled homes. Anyone who travels in Anglican circles in Africa and Asia cannot miss them: resplendent in their uniforms, lifting their voices in joyful song, or hard at work.

In both East and West Africa and in Polynesia, the Mothers' Union has been in the forefront, providing hostels for girls who have left their secure homes to work and study in large cities. One of the missionary dioceses in Northern Nigeria was sponsored by the Mothers Union of one of the Southern dioceses in its formative years, while some years ago in the Diocese of Mokono in Uganda, the women literally laid the foundations and built with their own bare hands a healthcare facility for children.

Most of these women often have little or no interest in being ordained; their cry is, "Just let us be free to serve the living God!" Although they may be enthusiastic about and supportive of the ordination of women, for many of them there are far more ways to serve than ordination.

Unfortunately, women were grievously under-represented at the G-CODE gathering, but when they spoke they did so with great power and dignity. The Rev. Elizabeth Kamau is a priest in the Church of the Province of Kenya. She told her audience one evening, "The men will not let us have the pulpits, they are afraid of losing their last post. Everywhere we are in charge — in the homes, in the schools, in refugee camps, in maternities, and naming (Christening) ceremonies, in hospitals and at funerals. There is only one preacher on one pulpit at one time. But wherever you turn women are busy, patiently and tirelessly teaching, guiding, comforting, healing. In short, bringing the presence and life of God to everyone." Her listeners' applause was thunderous!

Women are represented in disproportionate numbers in the churches almost everywhere, though in many places they are at the heart of the churches' life. Women are fervent in prayer, fearless in proclamation, patiently loving, and are often the visionaries and the pioneers of exciting new ministries. That women are so predominant is something for which we can, on the one hand, thank God, and on the other offer a challenge to males!

Reaching out to the young is indispensable. At G-CODE it was affirmed again and again that the youth are the church's greatest asset, our best hope for the future. It was Nigeria's young men and women whom God visited, giving them the vision that has led that enormous church forward, when their elders had somehow missed the turn. Everywhere today the young are courted by advertisers and a global entertainment industry that wants to make them in its own image. The tragedy is that we seem unwilling to invest in the young — time, treasure, talent, and ourselves. Churches that minister effectively to the young will, no doubt, be greatly blessed. We fear for the very survival of those who do not.

7. *Growing Churches are Rooted in Scripture:*

Again and again at the G-CODE gathering, it became blatantly obvious that there is an organic relationship between reverence for the Scriptures and evangelistic progress. "We have no high theology," said Bishop Yong Ping Chung of Sabah. "We simply follow the Bible, and our churches keep growing." Our observations around the world corroborate this. Those churches which determine to be faithful to the Scriptures tend to grow, elsewhere; stagnation seem to be the primary fruit, the church having become "enslaved to what Alisdair MacIntyre refers to as the self-image of the age.'"[13]

Stephen Mungoma, Evangelism Officer of the Church of Uganda and a doctoral candidate at Fuller Theological Seminary in Pasadena, California, began his report to G-CODE by saying that "the Anglican Church in Uganda is committed to the Scriptures, to evangelism, which means bringing men and women to Jesus Christ." Lakshman Peiris from Sri Lanka noted that in his country, hampered as they are by guerrilla war in one area, a rising tide of Hindu fundamentalism in another, and intense opposition from Buddhist zealots elsewhere, growth in Christ can be seen in the parishes which take seriously the revealed faith and the Scriptures. Archbishop Carey, while rightly deploring intolerance and bigotry, called on Christians to test all they do in light of Scripture. "If this Decade of Evangelism is not a call to a historic and biblical faith it will be but a passing, ephemeral thing," Dr. Carey explained.[14]

Where there is confidence in the Gospel as revealed in Scripture, Christians are most likely to have an evangelistic heart, and an abiding missionary passion. When people are convinced that this Good News is relevant to today's world, and where there are no doubts about the eternal consequences of the death and resurrection of Jesus Christ, and his identity as the divine Son of God, churches are either holding their own or, even in the face of opposition or bloody persecution, forging ahead and meeting the yearnings of a spiritually hungry humanity.

The reasons for this are evident. Not only does such a red-blooded understanding of the faith stand in stark contrast to the increasing secularization of popular Western culture, but it also clearly delineates the differences between believers and adherents of other religions, especially where Christianity is a minority movement. Detractors will suggest that such a bold and forthright faith "evades the real issues and offers cheap and easy fixes to complex problems."[15] However, it is because biblical Christianity is realistic, grounded in God's self-revelation, that it has the capacity not only to speak to the deepest longings of the human soul, but also to address the apparently intransigent issues troubling our shrinking world.

The truth is that wherever the church has not surrendered to what one theologian has called "Christological heart failure," there is a commitment to evangelism and mission. In many cases this commitment is leading to significant growth — and robust spiritual health.

8. *Growing Churches are Thinking Churches with a Clear Apologetic:*

Listening to passionate evangelists talk, observing where successful evangelistic ministry is taking place, and reading the reports of evangelistic enterprises around the world, it is obvious that those committed to the evangelistic task have usually thought long and hard about the nature of the world into which they are projecting their message, so that they can speak the message of Christ relevantly to it. Understanding the environment in this way profoundly influences how the message is presented. Not only is the Gospel shown to be something eminently rational, but those presenting it are willing to respect the doubts of those feeling toward the faith. Indeed, they see such misgivings as a potential springboard to genuine belief — the camel's nose poking through the tent flap of someone's spiritual life.

Apologetics, the business of defending the faith and presenting its intellectual challenge, is the art of beginning where people are. "If evangelism is like offering someone bread," write Alister McGrath and Michael Green, "apologetics is about persuading people that there is bread on offer, and that it is good to eat."[16] McGrath and Green go on to point out that if evangelism offers people faith in Christ, apologetics stresses the attractiveness of that offer.

Holy Trinity, Brompton's, Alpha Course has bonded thoughtful apologetic with the attractive offer of salvation in Jesus Christ. With its emphasis on small groups, friendly shared meals, and inviting the unchurched to share their personal experiences as well as their deepest questions, Alpha attempts to steer those who are spiritually hungry and fumbling after belief, toward a well-rounded understanding of Christianity. This in turn becomes a life-changing experience — without bypassing people's brains. Nicholas Gumbel, one of the leaders of the Course and a priest on the staff of Holy Trinity, describes it as "an effective evangelistic program, returning evangelism to where it started — the parish church."[17]

Effective apologetics are rooted in a Christian tradition with a rich and inquisitive intellectual life. Gifted apologists marry the art of rational persuasion with the power of the Gospel. They demonstrate that the Good News, far from being irrelevant, as many post-Christian people believe, speaks to the *ennui* of secular men and women, as well as the yearnings of those whose cultures have been shared by other forces, religions, and superstitions. Apologetics requires believers to be students and observers of every facet of the environment in which they live, as well as the truths and the implications of their faith. Objections are to be taken seriously, and the mind has to be treated as a vital part of the whole person.

When all this happens, exciting and life-changing evangelism takes place. Growing congregations respect the intelligence of inquirers after truth, and work hard to proclaim and live out the faith in such a way that it makes eminent sense to those who are searching.

9. Growing Churches are Caring Churches:

Contrary to popular misconceptions, evangelistic churches are not glorified scalp-hunting operations. Growing churches are almost always interested in a great deal more than the good of people's souls. While we have devoted a considerable number of pages to the priority of the verbal presentation of the message, words are meaningless if they are divorced from care, love, and humble Christian service.

In countries where evangelism through open presentation of the Gospel is difficult, it has been through hospitals, clinics, and other social welfare and care institutions that the churches have been able to represent their Lord to the people around them. This is particularly so in much of the Arab world, where even into this century the church, once numerically strong, has now dwindled as a result of emigration or hostility from the majority community. As one Arab Christian has put it, through various caring agencies Christians build bridges and demolish walls between themselves and the Islamic population. In some places, literally tens of thousands turn to Christian clinics for basic health-care every year. "Our church has big arms in its institutions," he said.

No one can accurately measure the influence institutions are having on the lives of those for whom they care. Yet a local Arab leader, following a stay in a Christian hospital, affirmed wholeheartedly the care he had been given: "I have known nothing but hatred, war, and distrust all my life, but now you have shown me that love is nobler and stronger than hatred. Thank you." We can only guess at the long-term cumulative impact of Christian compassion.

The church in the Arab world, limited in its avenues for forthright proclamation, witnesses primarily through its institutions — and other opportunities for humble service which present themselves. But in other places ministries of concern grow out of the local congregation as all around it encounters disease, pain, racism, marginalization, and dreadful suffering as a result of various forms of dehumanization.

"We carry the hoe in one hand and the Bible in the other," said a development officer in Kenya, as he showed off the tea plantation and the "zero grazing" project he had helped a group of new converts to Christ set up. It is such a holistic view of mission that brings us to a far richer understanding of every facet of Christian witness and which constitutes dynamic evangelism and make for genuine growth.

Throughout East Africa, the churches play a leading role in the fight against AIDS. Medical detectives are not entirely sure how HIV found its way into the human population, and which is having a devastating impact on many African countries.[18] As many as one in ten Ugandans carry the infection, the disease having left 1.5 million orphans. The church not only provides health-care education, but (as far as its resources will allow) goes to the aid of those who have fallen victim to this plague — and their grieving children. These are overwhelming challenges which Anglican, Catholic, and other churches are doing their best to address. These efforts, hindered by Uganda's poverty, were exacerbated by the dictatorships of Idi Amin and Milton Obote — and the military campaigns which eventual removed them.

Stephen Mungoma illustrated the interplay of forces which create opportunities for holistic ministry, when he spoke of evangelism being "by the whole church for the whole person." With great passion and compassion he went on: "The whole person means that we are not just here to save souls." As he spoke of the AIDS crisis and its impact on his country, he also drew attention to the way socio-economic circumstances make matters worse. While Uganda's external debt of $5 billion is relatively modest when put alongside the sums owed by Western nations, to Uganda it is crippling. The nation's struggles have been complicated by the manner in which the world's richer nations depressed the price of coffee on the world market, thereby devaluing the country's primary export — and reducing funds available to address the needs of the people. As complex as such international economic issues are, Stephen pointed out, the Gospel addresses them and Christians have a part to play in ensuring international fairness. Evangelism may be the sharpest end of Christian mission, but is just one part of a much larger picture.

St. Edmund's Church, Temple Hill, on the southeastern edge of

London, is set in the heart of a public housing project — what the British call a council estate. Since the beginning of the Decade of Evangelism the congregation has grown from 30 to more than 85 persons. This little Christian community in a difficult corner of England puts itself under the sovereignty of God, "with prayer as the foundation of all we do." At the heart of their evangelistic strategy is an open door policy which has enabled them to reach out to those often shunned by the church: gay men and lesbians, the divorced, and those who are society's outcasts, for example. "However," writes the Vicar, "although we welcome, we never compromise the gospel." Perhaps this little parish illustrates the importance of unconditional love, although there is a heartbreaking side to such generosity, with many falling away from the faith. "The parable of the sower has been a key to understanding church life," the priest explains.

If our churches are to reflect the love of Christ in its fullness, and live out the cost of discipleship, then evangelism cannot stand "aloof from matters of justice and human welfare which does not reflect adequately the biblical revelation... Proclamation and service are seen as belonging together (and) the (Anglican) Communion is encouraged to become a missionary body whose activities go beyond pastoral care and nurture."[19]

10. Growing Churches have a Global Vision:

There are "four roads from the altar" for the Church of the Good Samaritan in Paoli, Pennsylvania. They have built their mission around Jesus's final charge to go out into "Jerusalem, Judea, Samaria, and the uttermost parts of the earth."[20] They put flesh on the bones of this text by involving themselves in a variety of local ministries (Jerusalem); focusing on specific ministries within the Diocese of Pennsylvania (Judea); working cross-culturally within the USA (Samaria); and then supporting the work of cross-cultural ministries and missionaries in various parts of the world. By setting up their outreach in this way, each ministry has fed and stimulated the others.

Churches which have a passion to engage in evangelism in their own communities usually realize that they have a responsibility to share the message in all the world. We should not be surprised that the healthy, growing churches of Africa, despite their lack of material resources, are now establishing ways to enable themselves to send people out beyond their own ethnic and national boundaries to be heralds of the Gospel. Various regional groups talked about this at some length at the G-CODE gathering, we are likely to see the fruits of these discussions in coming years. A foretaste of this growing global vision among the African churches can be seen in the purpose statement of the Anglican Evangelistic Association in Tanzania, which lists among its primary objectives, "To help rekindle living faith in the churches of the Anglican Communion... (and) to preach the Gospel to all people."[21]

The Diocese of Chile, young as it is, already has two missionary families working with the Reformed Episcopal Church in Spain — and more are likely to follow. Still in South America, the Diocese of Argentina, whose see city is Buenos Aires, has a full-time lay evangelist who not only leads missions throughout Argentina and provides evangelistic training, but is also being used increasingly around the world. Those young "missionary dioceses" in Northern Nigeria, despite the huge challenges facing them on their own doorsteps, are already laying plans to expand their ministry into Chad, Niger, and Burkina Faso. They also want to form links with the Sudan, in order to help the war-ravaged church there to train leaders and clergy.

While this new surge of energy is beginning to flow, older churches, like the Episcopal Church in the USA and the Anglican Church in Canada, have tended to lose their way when it comes to global ministry. Given their own domestic stagnation and decline, this should not surprise us. Nevertheless, a fresh vision to spread the Gospel to the ends of the earth is emerging in the North American church, support for which is rooted in the healthiest, liveliest parishes.[22]

Researchers, like David Barrett, constantly remind us that hundreds of millions remain unreached by the Gospel, and Christians of all stripes and traditions — including Anglicans — have got to use their ingenuity and explore every kind of new method to get the message out. With the tools, the tenacity, and the sacrificial commitment, the dream first expressed by Christians in the late Nineteenth Century is not beyond our reach: "The evangelization of the world in our generation."

However, Westerners will only be a small part of tomorrow's

missionary force. We are starting to see a delicious mish-mash of people who are bound from everywhere to everywhere, "gossiping the gospel" as they go. In this new age of missions we need to learn how to share gifts and resources, including the benefits and drawbacks of our various ethnicities. Anglicans, belonging as we do to a worldwide communion, are in a position to explore all the permutations, and modern communications should enable this. To illustrate this recently an invitation offered to American parishes to develop a partner parish relationship with a congregation of the Russian Orthodox Church, was picked up by an archdeacon in Kenya who immediately wrote asking for a sister parish in Russia for his own congregations![23]

Given communications and travel possibilities opening up to increasing numbers everywhere, the first century of the third millennium of the Christian era could see a re-energized vision for global mission sweeping through the churches. Anglicans would make a formidable Christian "army" if we can find ways to unite the spirituality and vibrancy of the younger churches with the heritage and material resources of the older, more established ones.

11. Growing Churches are Willing to Make Changes:

As we prepare for a new century and new millennium, a full-scale mobilization of the People of God for ministry is vital, if we are to be effective. The task of leaders, lay and ordained, both now and in the years ahead, is to create the environment in which people can be formed in Christ, discover how God has gifted them, and then enable them to live our their discipleship in a world which is exhilarating, bewildering, and at the same time altering at breakneck speed.

All this spells a willingness to make radical changes when and where necessary. While every effort must be made to preserve what is good and has lasting value in our tradition, we also need to be willing to discard or alter whatever stands in the way of effective evangelism and spiritual health. Making the right changes in the right way can be precarious, but the secret of enabling growth is managing change.[24]

When Chairman Mao Tse-Tung was riding high in the People's Republic of China, there was excited talk of "continuous revolution" from the cadres who did his bidding. Maybe the challenge before us, as we look beyond the Decade of Evangelism, is how we can always be ready to recognize and take the opportunities a changing world is forcing upon us. Because of the mammoth cultural shifts that are likely to continue into the foreseeable future, we must discover how to maintain freshness of vision and willingness to avoid getting stuck in a rut.

Times of massive change are times of extraordinary opportunity. One former Presbyterian missionary, after long and careful observation of the way the world is being remade, puts it this way: "The colliding waves of change, when one era is coming to an end and a new one is about to begin, can be seen as the hidden activity of God."[25]

◆ ◆ ◆ ◆ ◆

Holy Spirit of God,
all powerful as the wind
you came to the Church on the Day of Pentecost
to quicken its life and empower its witness.
Come to us now as the Wind of Heaven
and breath new life into our souls;
and revive your work among us,
that God in all things may be glorified,
through Jesus Christ our Lord. Amen

What we have said:

■ Evangelistic churches are almost always growing churches.

■ Churches which take evangelism seriously, pray seriously and look to God to answer their prayers.

■ Growing churches have a rich worship life, yet are sensitive to the needs of outsiders.

■ Effective evangelism is usually guided by strong, visionary leadership and a firm hold on the formularies of the faith as found in Scripture.

■ Apologetics are taken seriously by those who take evangelism, mission, and church growth seriously.

■ Christian compassion and evangelism belong together and often lead to growth.

■ Growing churches have a healthy global vision.

■ Being willing to change is one of the "life signs" of a healthy evangelistic church and a source of hope for the future.

Thinking it over:

■ Give some thought to the ways in which you can intensify the prayer life of your parish, rooting it in the evangelistic calling.

■ What are the qualifications you think you would look for in a priest who is going to be one of the leaders of an evangelistic or growing congregation?

■ Can you identify the characteristics of a growing, evangelistic church that your parish both possesses and lacks?

■ Does your church's worship help outsiders over the threshold, or does it hinder them from coming in?

■ Is your congregation willing to make major changes in order to be more effective in outreach?

CHAPTER TEN
The Challenges That Face Us

"Evangelism is a dangerous business." — WALTER HOLLENWEGER

The Christian churches in North Africa were once among the most exciting in the world, yet all that remains of them today are the silent ruins of their once splendid buildings. The heroes of the African churches, the likes of Augustine of Hippo and Cyprian, are unremembered and unhonored by the Muslim descendants of those Christians they once led.

Like large chunks of Central Asia, North Africa is the Land of the Vanished Church. At the beginning of this century, one in three people living in Turkey were at least nominally Christian, today there are less than 5,000 left in the whole land. Over this huge area echoes the call of the minaret.

The fate of North African Christianity stands as a warning to those incapable or unwilling to grasp the signs of the times. We cannot afford to under-estimate the challenges and obstacles before us. Arrogant, divided, and out of touch, those African churches were in such a parlous state that when Islam swept out of Arabia, they were quickly shoved to one side. It took just a few generations for them to be almost totally submerged. Such is the fate of a church which had a large following, strong individual leadership, and unrestrained exuberance, but which had lost its anchor in the soil of its own culture. For church growth and ministry to stand the test of time, they require a firm theological and creedal undergirding; they must maintain a clear link with catholicity, and be rooted in its context in a non-syncretistic manner.

The challenges and obstacles to evangelism are enormous and numerous. Indeed, we have so much material dealing with this topic that we could probably write another book about this alone! Our mission has cosmic implications: we are in the business of retaking territory that the Evil One assumes now belongs to him. Talking to the veteran evangelists and missioners who gathered in North Carolina in September 1995, we heard in no uncertain terms how in their evangelistic work they struggle "not against flesh and blood but against principalities and powers."[1] The environment within which we work is made no easier by this rapid procession of change which is altering the whole face of this planet, erasing much that is familiar but not yet replacing it with something either better or more durable. Whatever emerges, the truth is that we are and will remain "resident aliens."

At its most extreme, the opposition we encounter when we proclaim the faith might well be hazardous to our health! Each year, tens of thousands of believers receive physical and psychological injuries which leave them permanently scarred, while Christian martyrdom has been the "growth industry" of the Twentieth Century. Since 1900 more believers have been put to death because of their faith than in any other period of history. Every day it is estimated that an average of 500 Christians are put to death because of their commitment to Jesus Christ. Most of them would not have died if they had kept their mouths shut and their faith to themselves: when taken seriously, evangelism really can put Christians in extreme danger. Even if martyrdom is unlikely to come our way, in every age effective Christian witnesses receive more than their fair share of ridicule from detractors and cultured despisers.

In this chapter we will see that the challenges come from both outside and within ourselves.

1. Lack of Urgency

"Maranatha, Come Lord Jesus," was a prayer constantly on the lips of early Christians. This sense of the imminence of Christ's return added urgency to their pursuit of the evangelistic task.

Fanning outward from Jerusalem, within a generation Christians could be found at the farthest reaches of the Roman Empire — and beyond. The tradition that India was evangelized by St. Thomas is deeply cherished by the Mar Thoma Church. Even if the apostle Thomas did not reach India, the tentacles of the Christian faith were probably probing that distant sub-continent within a couple of generations of Christ's death and resurrection.

Urgency seldom characterizes much of the church's mission today. Maybe because the Lord has tarried these two thousand years we sometimes wonder whether he will return at all. Or perhaps it is that we have allowed our busyness with "churchy" things to take precedence over the ministry of proclamation, Christ's parting words going unheeded as a result. While the younger churches might be less prone to this malaise, it is endemic where the faith has been known for centuries. Could it be that this indifference is borne of familiarity — or maybe it is that even those who claim an abiding commitment to Christ are not entirely sure that faith in him has eternal consequences? If we are to recovery the early church's sense of urgency, we need to recover confidence in the Gospel and its eternal implications.

2. The Corrosive Impact of Secularity

Then, despite the deepening spiritual hunger obvious everywhere on earth, there is the inexorable spread of secularity, packaged in a fast-expanding global popular culture whose messengers have the resources to take it to the world's remotest corners. As a result, the secular mind-set is inexorably invading new places, forcing increasing numbers to live their lives against its deadening backdrop. A good deal of our apathy about the proclamation of the Gospel is probably related to secularism's inroads makes into our own consciousness, and the subliminal manner in which it erodes our confidence in the uniqueness and the consequences of Christ's claims. This certainty is further damaged when prominent church leaders seem rather too eager to air their own misgivings in public, even going so far as attacking the veracity of the faith they have committed to uphold.

There is plenty to encourage detractors. They rub their hands with glee, believing the churches to be on a losing streak. Yet like the shepherd boy, David, we are armed with five apparently harmless smooth stones, which in the long term can and will deal a lethal blow to secularity! Seemingly out-gunned by the Philistine, nimbleness and the Spirit of the Lord were with David.[2] The Enlightenment, whose belief in "the omnicompetence of human reason"[3] has shaped Western culture and numbed our spirituality, is rapidly losing potency. We are moving into a time when the spiritual and the unseen have new meaning and significance. Our five smooth stones of faith have power to the uttermost if men and women of faith will rise up and use them in the name of the Lord God of hosts.

From his Oxford vantage point, the Principal of Wycliffe Hall tells us that secularism's twin, materialism, "is deeply vulnerable at the moment." As we seek to present the Christian faith as a viable alternative to secularity, there is now "a window of opportunity which those concerned with Christian renewal must make the most of." He goes on to ponder that "it is perhaps no accident that periods of growth in the Church often seem linked with economic decline. The proclamation of the Gospel today meets with a sympathy which would have been unimaginable at the height of the economic boom of less than a decade ago. Is it an accident that the Decade of Evangelism coincides with a period of economic depression?"[4]

But even as it fades, secularity is still in a position to do extensive damage — perhaps it has saved the worst until last. The shiny newness of materialism and accompanying worldliness is extraordinarily seductive, captivating whole populations the world over as dozens of new television channels vie for their attention. While rejoicing in the confidence of those Christians who are seeing God at work in extraordinary ways, we feel compelled to hoist the storm warning, "Let the one who stands beware lest he fall."

Many Western churches are just beginning to come to terms with the fact that much of their potency has been sapped because they have allowed themselves to be coopted by a secularism hostile to the faith. Meanwhile the ground beneath the churches in other parts of the planet is being eroded by the same secular forces for the first time — and in these places it appears that many Christians are under-estimating the damage secularism might do. We rejoice with those who are seeing great fruit as they proclaim the Gospel, but they have to be warned that they are no more immune from the ravages of secularism than their Western sisters and brothers.   Accelerating this secular spread is the continuing rapid globalization of the mass media.   While they are right to celebrate the power of God's Spirit in their midst, non-Western churches would be remiss to ignore forces capable of sucking them into the same black hole which has decimated churches in North America, Australasia and Europe.

3. The Challenge of the Cities

The world in which we live is becoming ever more urban. A million newcomers pour into the world's cities *every week*. During the early 1990s, an unnoticed milestone came and went when an unknown individual trudged from the countryside into a burgeoning city somewhere in Asia, Africa, or perhaps Latin America, and for the first time in human history more than 50% of the world's population had become urban dwellers. Cities must be more central to our evangelistic strategies, because they are set to shape the lives of urbanites and rural dwellers more and more.

In many places, these expanding metropolitan areas are not necessarily comfortable places in which to live. Infrastructures whose design limits might have been 5 million, are trying to serve perhaps three times that number, while the human surge from the rural areas shows no sign of abating. In many parts of the world housing is stretched to the limits, and uncounted numbers of people are living in gutters, on sidewalks, or in unsanitary hovels — often within sight of the palatial — but securely guarded, homes of the well-to-do. Encircling cities in more prosperous parts of the world are sprawling suburbs, where families seek to live out the middle class dream. Yet even the suburbs provide no refuge from human misery. Battered by the rising cost of living, family breakdown, violence, and every kind of substance abuse, millions of affluent suburbanites live out lives which are a nightmare of quiet desperation. Meanwhile in their midst the declining inner cities, which the affluent have abandoned, have been turned into what some are calling "little Third Worlds."

Cities have always been the crossroads of the world — not just for goods and services, but also for ideas and beliefs. This is something which was well understood by the Apostle Paul. As a result, it was Paul's strategy to focus on urban centers, realizing that if congregations that could reproduce themselves were planted there, they would be able to export their faith into the surrounding countryside. The way the Gospel spread throughout the Roman world is evidence that this strategy worked well.

Although our world is very different from Paul's, cities are even more crucial today, so perhaps it would be wise to shape our own strategy on his. Metropolitan areas are massive concentrations of resources, many of which, if committed to Christ's service, could be used fruitfully for evangelism and the mission of Christ. Too often in the past we have tended to focus disproportionate attention on rural areas, hoping that eventually the benefits would trickle into the cities. When the Gospel does travel in this direction, there are many more barriers to be crossed.

Today's cities and mega-cities anchor almost every global network in existence. They are the creators and consumers of the largest bulk of the world's education, health-care, trade and industry, and are focal points for travel and telecommunications. The wealthiest and most influential people are to be found in cities, as well as the vast majority of the dispossessed.

The challenge of urban mission and ministry is so great that Christians often balk at their challenge. In our general distaste for cities, we tend to opt for the tactics of survival in the urban wastelands, rather than develop strategies for advance. As a result we relegate ourselves to the margins or, put another way, we suburbanize and neutralize the church, thus missing extraordinary God-given opportunities. Instead of interpreting cities as heaving masses of humanity from which to escape, perhaps we should consider them as exciting challenges for world evangelization.[5]

4. The Inadequacy of Our Prayer

This is so important that it bears repeating: communities are most effectively evangelized by praying churches. Prayerlessness and the powerlessness of so many of our ecclesial structures and agencies are clearly closely related. In our observation, there is a definite linkage between prayer and mission. When prayer ebbs away, then so does the evangelistic effectiveness of congregations and whole churches.

Perhaps the most extraordinary facet of layperson Ronnie Lieu En Khiam and his work in the disenfranchised areas of

Kotakinabalu, Sabah, is not so much the signs and wonders which accompany it, but the volumes of prayer in which his work is soaked. Ronnie will talk nonchalantly about the prayer which accompanies his ministry in the context of any given situation, but when prompted to talk more about it, it becomes clear that this is far more than a collect from the Prayer Book, or even a ten minute bowing of heads. Often he and his co-workers will fast and wrestle before God for days before they sense they are ready to approach a fresh challenge.

There is an umbilical cord which joins prayer and evangelism in the life of the church. Too often it is either dangerously fragile or has been cut. The result is ministries which may have extraordinary form, even enormous human and material assets, but the parish or organization is absolutely impotent because it is starved of the nourishment which comes from that most mysterious of all resources, fervent, believing prayer. Here's the advice of one experienced prayer warrior: "Allow yourself and your church to take prayer as seriously as you take education, worship, outreach, and fellowship. The resulting outpouring of prayer will enrich all your ministries with God's vision and power."[6]

As we have seen, there has been an encouraging rediscovery of the power of intercessory prayer in recent years, but despite this our intercessory life remains very patchy. Great conferences, like the G-CODE 2000 gathering, are covered by teams of people struggling before God in prayer, but how many parishes and church institutions receive the same attention? Our plans and strategies are too often developed on the basis of expediency rather than being the outcome of an earnest search for God's will and purpose.

While realizing that prayer is often difficult to measure, the lack of it becomes very apparent very rapidly — as the gaping holes in many of our ministries point out. "If the intercessors God has placed in each congregation would be recognized, coordinated, and released for ministry, churches across... the world would be completely turned around. Unfortunately, many Christians, including pastors, do not realize that the intercessors are there, nor are they equipped to recognize them."[7] It would appear that the challenge to prayerfulness is an enormous one!

5. Disunity

It is hardly an accident that the ecumenical movement was nurtured in the great missionary movement as it accelerated forward during the latter part of the Victorian era. As Christians became more intentional in mission and evangelism, they discovered that the divisions they were exporting marred their witness to outsiders. Dissent among believers calls into question the credibility of the Church's proclamation, whether we are talking about unfortunate relationships within local congregations or tensions between denominational bodies. Because disagreement and conflict are so much part of the human condition, since the beginning the church has sought to resolve it, whether with councils like that called in Jerusalem to handle the conundrums raised by the arrival of Gentiles in the church (Acts 15), or urgings like Paul's that the dispute in Phillipi between Euodia and Syntyche be cleared up.[8]

There will always be differing streams of thought and distinct traditions within Christianity, and much of the time there is no reason why those with diverse emphases should not be able to cooperate with one another for the sake of God's mission. While it is impossible to quantify the damage done by strife or an uncooperative spirit among Christians, it clearly hurts their cause. A survey undertaken in the USA among secular people revealed the startling evidence that a majority of outsiders said they had enough problems of their own already, and as a result did not wish to join a church.

But disunity has wider implications than whether Christians agree among themselves or not. Where Christians are not talking for some reason or another, coordination of strategies and the deployment of resources is impossible. For example, there is very little linkage between the 23 plans established by those denominational and interdenominational groups who have made the 1990s a decade of evangelism. The outcome is that money and talent are wasted because of duplication of effort, while potentially fruitful fields for mission and evangelism are overlooked or missed altogether.

More than 150 years ago, the Rev. Anthony Grant, the 1843 Bampton Lecturer at Oxford University, said, "The past missionary efforts of the Church, when viewed in reference to the extensive and varied tracts of heathenism that lie before us, can be deemed only as inceptive and experimental. They resemble but the essays of the messengers sent to make trial of the land of promise, to ascertain the character of its natives, and bring back the first-fruits of its produce. A more organized movement, resolute and concentrated action, will be required...."[9] It seems the churches have yet to heed this advice.

6. *Inadequate Vision and Strategies*

The new world order which has started to emerge, and which is likely to continue unfolding until well into the next century, is presenting a host of opportunities for evangelism which we would not have dared to imagine just a few years ago. The Enlightenment consensus in the West is crumbling and people are genuinely curious about things spiritual, while doors which until recently were tightly closed are now opening for mission. Technologies are also increasingly available which, if properly used, can help us fulfill our ministry. Some Christians are grasping today's opportunities with both hands, while for others this is a terrifying time and they have backed themselves into "safe" positions.

Times like these are times of opportunity when God is calling upon believers to exercise their vision and imagination as they seek to make Christ known to an unbelieving world. Many Christians seem totally incapable of breaking out of yesterday's molds and structures, and exploring fresh approaches to outreach and evangelism which would in many instances be far more profitable. Someone has suggested that the seven last words of a church that is mired in the past are probably "We've never done it that way before!" The Archbishop of Canterbury has challenged us to take seriously the "gift of risk taking, of risking failure," if the Great Commission is to be fulfilled in our generation.

We are not saying that all the rich fruits of our heritage should be sacrificed on the altar of innovation. We are convinced that a healthy faith is one which is rooted and grounded in its past, but we should be willing to listen to those voices, often coming from the fringes, which are telling us that there are different and more relevant ways of doing things and presenting Christ. At the same time we need to be willing to carefully examine our present approaches and be prepared to discard them if it is clear that they hinder the presentation of the Gospel and the incorporation of new Christians. Vehicles which once may have worked, in the world which is emerging may very well have become totally unproductive. Keeping an ineffective organization running or carrying on with programs from which there are decreasing returns, when the resources could be used more effectively elsewhere, is tantamount to a declaration of intent to commit suicide.

This unwillingness to make changes plays into the natural human tendency to filter from our consciousness the bad and the failed, and instead to focus on the good and successful. We certainly do this when publicizing mission work and the results of our evangelistic ministries. Our minds are almost programmed to be selective, highlighting those things which have gone well, while downplaying or even refusing to report our failures. Sadly, part of the reason for this is that funding for our work may be dependent on something donors can interpret as "success."

Too many ministries around the church try to bury their failures rather than analyze what went wrong. The result of this denial is that the same mistakes are then repeated further down the road, or work which would be extremely valuable if it was fine-tuned is prematurely abandoned because we interpret the necessary digging of foundations as failure. We say it again: times of radical change are times of enormous opportunity. Do we have the vision to see the possibilities and ride the wave of change? We may need to refit ourselves if we are to get across the changing landscape, and hard as that might be, the outcome will bring great glory to God.

7. Failure to Do the Legwork

Evangelistic enterprises fail for any number of reasons. The approach might be inappropriate, prayer backing sparse, or the strategy being pursued has been inadequately thought out or tested. Some of our shortcomings will only be discovered "in the heat of battle," but others could have been avoided if churches had been more intentional and careful in their preparations.

An impartial observer at the G-CODE 2000 Conference, able to listen to every presentation, sit in on every group, or eavesdrop on every conversation, would have reached the conclusion that those people who were succeeding in evangelism and missionary outreach were those who had clear goals, a well planned strategy with short, medium, and long-term objectives, and a humble recognition that any advance they made was by the power of the Holy

Spirit. Churches which lacked these things might have been rich in resources, but they were, generally, poor in results. Obviously, the goals and objectives in various parts of the world will be different. Those living out their faith in the midst of the Islamic world or Japan, will not have the same expectations numerically as those in Mozambique, Tanzania, or Nigeria.

All evangelistic activity should be accompanied by thorough planning and preparation. The tendency is always there to fall into the temptation of cutting these corners, either because we are impatient, or because we think it might save a little money — something which is almost always in short supply in the church's ministry of proclamation. Rushing along, we might overlook the importance of gathering and processing data, and, instead make far-reaching decisions on the basis of a hunch. As important as intuition is, unless it is educated by solid information, it is very easy for Christians to find themselves going off tangentially.

8. Failure to Make Proclamation a Priority

Perhaps the major obstacle to the spread of the Gospel is the ability of the churches to make everything but the proclamation of Christ a priority. This is not just a problem facing the older, historically more established churches of the West, it can happen everywhere. Within a generation, a vibrant, excited group of Gospel-sharers can turn themselves into a comfortable, ingrown community, congratulating themselves on the beauty of their liturgy or the eloquence of their priest.

Maybe one of the greatest weaknesses of Christians in general, and Anglicans in particular, is their desire to be perceived as respectable. When respectability becomes pre-eminent, the forthright forthtelling of the faith is usually the first victim, and tends to be toned down. While little is gained from being unnecessarily offensive in the way we present the faith, the exclusivity of Christ's claims upon the hearts and souls of men and women cannot be minimized so that it is made more palatable. The Gospel's claims are no excuse for rudeness, but as damaging as unnecessary pushiness might be, side-stepping the heart of our message's substance does even more harm in the long term.

Some provinces of the Anglican Communion have so shunted proclamation to the margins that without radical structural change it would be difficult for the evangelistic task to be restored to its rightful place as the primary focus of the church's life. These provinces might be giving inordinate attention to areas of ministry which may be extraordinarily legitimate, but they are building on sand if they do little to draw new believers into Christ's Kingdom. In other provinces, the agendas of the church have become so garbled that evangelistic ministry is even frowned upon, re-interpreted, or openly discouraged.

Where this is the case, the Lands of the Vanished Churches mentioned at the start of this chapter stand as a warning to us. A church which shies away from the Great Commission, or gets lost in other agendas, will itself become a mission field within a few generations — and all over the world we are seeing this happen while Christians stand by bemused, and perhaps a little bewildered.

Yet there is always the prevailing sense that God has not finished with his church yet. It might have turned itself into Ezekiel's Valley of Dry Bones, but again and again we have seen God's Spirit swoop in to transform that desolation into a praising, rejoicing, witnessing community of people. Then over the years these newly-fired Christians have taken the tired structures and made them live once more. This is happening today in the West, in Africa, in parts of Asia, indeed almost everywhere.

◆ ◆ ◆ ◆

Heavenly Father,
You who spared yourself nothing in order to come and serve us
who owe you everything;
Rekindle in our hearts a flame of sacred love,
A renewed awe for the eternal consequences of the Gospel
And fire us with the zeal and sense of urgency
that its proclamation demands.
Fill us with your Holy Spirit, in humility, holiness, confidence,
And vigor to proclaim the Good News
of your love and ultimate judgment,
Till the whole earth is filled with your glory,
"As the waters cover the sea." Amen

What we have said:

■ The call of the Gospel demands an unconditional self-giving.

■ There are many challenges which stand in the way of effective Christian witness in the world today.

■ Secularism is loosening its grip on the Western mind-set and consequently there is deep spiritual hunger.

■ We need to recover confidence in the relevance of the Gospel for today — and its eternal consequences.

■ We need to recover the sense of urgency which the Great Commission implies.

■ Prayer, the deep outpouring of the soul and spirit by importunate humans, "prostrate" before the holy and almighty God, is crucial to the success of our evangelistic task.

Thinking it over:

■ In some places persecution is violent, barbaric and sometimes leads to physical martyrdom; in others it is more subtle and cultured. Discuss what this means in respect to the West.

■ What challenges face wholehearted evangelism in your area, and how are you going to deal with them?

■ Those who think they stand, should take heed lest they fall. The tragedy of the church in North Africa in the Seventh Century AD is a case in point. How do we avoid such tragedy today, and what should we do to secure the future of the rapidly growing church in the Two-Thirds World?

■ Confidence in the Gospel; a sense of urgency; awesomeness of a supremely loving but altogether just and holy God; eternal consequences of the Gospel; spirituality; prayer that comes from the heart; and prayer that comes from and returns to God, and that effects the will of God among humans... These phrases and ideas occur repeatedly in this chapter. How can you and your local church maintain/recover these in your Christian life and ministry?

CHAPTER ELEVEN
The Story Goes On...

"I cannot fail to recall the optimistic mood which I and many others felt when we considered the condition of the Reformed Churches in 1591.... We imagined that a golden age had dawned!"
— ABRAHAM SCULTETUS 1566-1624[1]

How Do You Conclude a Book Like This?

Vision Bearers is little more than a tiny fragment of a much bigger and longer tale. The story of evangelism is as old as the Christian church itself, and the work of evangelism will not end until that last moment of time. The ministry of evangelism will only be finished when the human story is finally over, Christ has returned, and the church militant is finally enfolded by God into the church triumphant. What we have told is a mere fragment of one full and very exciting chapter of this long adventure. We have used the Anglican Communion as the lens through which to look at what is going on all over the world, but the same joys and challenges are there in every other Christian tradition.

As in every other chapter of the history of the church, the results of its mission is patchy. In some places extraordinary progress is being made, in others ground is clearly being lost, while in yet other arenas the tide could clearly turn in either direction. We were putting the finishing touches to this manuscript in January 1996, when the Church of England published a report, *Signs of Life*, which confirmed that decline had bottomed out, while on average a new Anglican congregation is being planted somewhere in England each week. The smiling faces of Bishop Nigel McCulloch and Canon Bob Warren, the church's evangelism officer, appeared in at least one national newspaper in Britain saying, "These signs confound the doom and gloom merchants that the Church of England is on its last legs."[1]

We have written from the human perspective — which, admittedly, is a very limited angle from which to witness the whole sweep of God's work of salvation. There is a divine viewpoint, mysterious and yet very beautiful, of which we occasionally catch momentary glimpses. The One whose perspective this is, is the Lord of the church, whose will it is that we should be a missionary people.

As we find ourselves gazing into the future and wondering, there are many imponderables. We have no idea where the Spirit of God might light fresh fires of revival, or bring to life the Valley of Dry Bones[3] — often there is something unexpected about both these facets of God's involvement with us. The whole planet is altering every day, and the transition which began to shape up in the 1960s is accelerating. A new kind of world is being hurried into existence. During the next twenty or thirty years, the changeover is going to be so great that wherever on earth we happen to live, much of our lives are bound to be altered beyond recognition. Christians have a choice. Either they can go out and meet head-on this new world with all its challenges, or we can huddle in fear in our comfortable little cocoons, stagnate, become ever more irrelevant, and finally disappear.

We believe with all our hearts that this is God's moment for the church, frightening as it sometimes might seem. The new millennium which will soon be upon us is beckoning, persuading us to redouble our efforts to take the Good News to all people everywhere — that God came down among us to redeem all humankind. Far from being a time for timidity, this is *kairos*, God's Saving Moment. We do not apologize for repeating the words of that wise old American Presbyterian missionary, who pondered his past ministry a few years ago, then looked forward into the future. We do so because what he said needs to be read, learned, and inwardly digested by the Christian church: "The colliding waves of change, when one era is coming to an end and a new one is about to begin, can be seen as the hidden activity of God."[4]

Increasingly, God's hidden activity is not so hidden. Spiritual hunger is breaking out everywhere as people realize that their deepest yearnings will not be met by more goods and services — the Archbishop of Canterbury picked up on this in his 1996 New Year's message to the Anglican Communion. The political, environmental, and social challenges facing our planet are of such a magnitude that without diplomacy, intelligence, and intimate help from a greater Power than ourselves, we are likely to permanently destroy the ecosphere, threatening not just the future of the human race but of all life on "this fragile earth, our island home."[5]

Meanwhile, it is now possible for those at one end of the world to communicate with people living at the other in a way beyond imagining even a relatively short time ago. While the technology which makes this possible can be used to destroy the spiritual appetite and deaden the sensitivities of the heart by reinforcing the most crass materialism, it can also be used in remarkable ways to spread the Good News. Only last year, Billy Graham's evangelistic campaign in Puerto Rico was beamed to scores of countries all over the planet, and in a few days the aging (and ailing) evangelist spoke the Truth to more people than he had previously done in his whole long and fruitful lifetime — and this is just a foretaste of things to come.

There seem to have been only two other moments like this one in Christian history. The first was in the fourth and fifth centuries AD, when the faith was in the process of becoming the dominant religion of the Roman Empire, while the empire itself was on its last legs and a new social structure was being born. The second was that watershed in history we today know as the Renaissance and Reformation. Each was a time of enormous uncertainty coupled with extraordinary change — and so is our age.

While there was certainly wonderful missionary work carried out during the Dark Ages in Europe — we can talk of the exploits of St. Patrick, the Celtic church, the evangelization of Russia, for example, somehow something died within the church as it faced that challenge. The church, by and large, retreated into a cocoon of its own making, and despite various attempts to "jump start" it, the best part of a thousand years was to pass for the message to shake itself loose. On the other hand, the Renaissance set in motion events and the march of ideas that gave birth to a richer, fuller understanding of the power of the Gospel. The churches began to renew themselves in Europe, and the story which had been locked up there for so long started its triumphant journey to even the most remote areas of the planet.

Researcher and former CMS missionary, David B. Barrett, received a letter early in 1995 from some Christians in a Ugandan diocese. His correspondents were eager to get involved with people unreached by the Gospel, and were asking him if there were any people groups who had not been touched by the faith within a few days ride on a bicycle of their home. Dr. Barrett wrote back, thanked them for their interest in this kind of pioneer ministry, encouraged them to work and pray for the salvation of the world, but had to inform them that they had written to him 100 years too late! This touching incident illustrates the manner in which the Gospel, once planted in what had been alien soil, has spread so mightily as a result of the forces which came into play in the sixteenth century.

As another great chapter change in human history takes place before our very eyes, the churches are again at a crossroads. Are we going to follow the example of our fifth or our sixteenth century forebears?

On that great day when Christ sums all things up, the seer foresaw that members of every nation, tribe, ethnic group and tongue would be gathered around the throne.[6] This means the job before us is enormous. There are still thousands of ethnic groups who have yet to hear the message, vast tracts of land where there is no Christian church, and innumerable cities, towns, and villages bereft of Christian witness. At the same time, in places where once the church was strong and vibrant, it is now in a parlous state having lost its way and fumbled with the message. In some places, like the Land of the Vanished Church, it has almost disappeared altogether, and those people, who are actually the descendants of Christians, call out for a work of total re-evangelization.

In the quite recent past, Christians mistakenly concluded that the mission of going into all the world with the Gospel is now drawing to a close. While it is starting to look as if we are nearer the end than the beginning, this perception could be premature, to say the least. We are aware that there is still much to be done, and billions who have yet to have the chance to respond to the One who is our Lord and our Savior.

As the last century ended Christians were talking about the possibility of "the evangelization of the world in this generation." We applaud their optimistic enthusiasm and want to follow strenuously in their footsteps. What vision our forebears in the faith had! Whether the evangelization of the world in our generation is possible we do not know. Some missiologists are suggesting that what lies ahead is the most challenging leg of the task of world evangelization.[7] What we do know is that we are the ones God is calling to lay our all on the altar, lift high the cross, and follow the vision that challenges us to give all the opportunity to know Jesus Christ, whether they are our friends and neighbors, or whether they live in the folds of the Tibetan Himalayas.

Sisters and Brothers in Christ: Our Lord's call as we enter the new millenniun is to be *Vision Bearers*!

◆ ◆ ◆ ◆ ◆

Both authors want to thank you for reading *Vision Bearers*. We hope and pray that the book has not only been a blessing to you, but that it has enriched your understanding of how God is at work in the world today.

Should you want to communicate with us, know something more about our ministries, have either of us consider visiting you for missions, weekends, conferences, etc., we can be reached at the following addresses:

The Revd. Richard Kew
Russian Ministry Network
P. O. Box 2806
Murfreesboro, TN 37133-2806
United States of America

Phone: (1) (615) 849 1354
Fax: (1) (615) 848 9143
E-Mail: RichardKew@aol.com or
        RichardKew@XC.org

The Revd. Dr. Cyril C. Okorocha
The Anglican Communion
157 Waterloo Road
London SE1 8UT
United Kingdom

Phone: (44) 0171 620 1110
Fax: (44) 0171 620 1070
E-Mail: Cyril_Okorocha@ecunet.org

▌ *Notes*

CHAPTER ONE

1. In his book, *Evangelism That Works* (Ventura, CA: Regal Books, 1995), George Barna points out how important it is for congregations to use a variety of approaches to evangelism to reach different kinds of people.

2. Acts 8:1-7.

3. We are grateful to Donald L. Stahl for sharing this idea with us.

4. Archbishop George L. Carey, speaking at the Global Conference for Dynamic Evangelism beyond AD 2000 (G-CODE 2000), held at the Kanuga Conference Center, Hendersonville, NC, September 4-9, 1995.

5. Matthew 28:16-19.

CHAPTER TWO

1. Chinedu Nebo holds degrees and professorships in metallurgic engineering from both Nigerian and US universities.

2. The word "kleptocracy" is Dr. Nebo's own description of the manner in which so many African leaders rule their nations by robbing from them.

3. The leadership of the Anglican Communion met in England at the Lambeth Conference of Bishops in 1988, and recognized that "evangelism is the primary task given to the church, " by the risen Christ. By and large, the churches in the Two-Thirds World have responded dynamically, while those in the West have yet to wake up to this reality.

4. Quoted from the written report of the Anglican Evangelistic Association given to the G-CODE 2000 Conference.

5. "The Jesus Film" is estimated to have been seen by over 700 million people and has resulted in more than 40 million people committing themselves to Christ. It is a project of Campus Crusade for Christ based in Orlando, FL. In a chance conversation on a plane with a man who had worked in advertising in East Africa a number of years ago, we discovered that detergent companies used a similar method to sell their products in the 1960s and 1970s!

6. The Most Revd. Brian Davis, *The Way Ahead* (Christchurch, New Zealand: The Caxton Press, 1995), p. 47.

7. Details about the Alpha Course are available from Holy Trinity Church, Brompton Road, London SW 7 1JA, England. Phone: 0171 581 8255, Fax: 0171 589 3390, or in the USA from Truro Episcopal Church, 10520 Main Street, Fairfax, VA 22030, Phone: (703) 273-8686, Fax: (703) 591-0737.

8. The Vineyard Fellowship of Churches grew out of the "Jesus Movement" and the ministry of John Wimber in Southern California in the 1960s and has now spread throughout North America and other parts of the English speaking world.

9. Professor David Martin speaking to a public meeting of the Woking Deanery, Surrey, England, in 1995.

10. Diogenes Allen, quoted by George G. Hunter, III, in *How to Reach Secular People* (Nashville, TN: Abingdon Press, 1992), p. 54.

11. Lesslie Newbigin, *Unfinished Agenda* (London: SPCK, 1985), p. 249.

12. Cyril C. Okorocha (ed.), *Trumpet from the South: Resolutions and Recommendations of the First Anglican Encounter in the South*. This was a consultation on mission and leadership from the South held in Limuru, Kenya, February 1-6, 1994. *Trumpet from the South* is distributed by the Anglican Consultative Council, 157 Waterloo Rd., London SE1 8UT, England. The Chileans in Spain are part of a three-way partnership which involves Anglicans in Chile, Spain, and England's branch of the South American Missionary Society.

13. C. Peter Wagner, *Spreading the Fire* (Ventura, CA: Regal Books, 1994), p. 70.

14. David B. Barrett's News Commentary, *AD 2025 Global Monitor*, July/August 1995.

15. The progress of the spread of the Christian gospel, and a detailed breakdown of these statistics can be found in the *World Christian Encyclopedia* (Oxford University Press, 1983), edited by David B. Barrett, and in the *AD 2025 Global Monitor*, published bi-monthly by the GEM global monitoring network. A new edition of the *World Christian Encyclopedia* is slated for publication both traditionally and electronically in 1997. Early estimates suggest the cost of this invaluable resource will be $200-$300. For more information contact GEM@XC.org.

16. Anglican Frontier Missions, PO Box 18024, Richmond, VA 23226-8024. Phone: (804) 355-8468, Fax: (804) 355-8260. E-Mail: AFM@XC.org.

17. Matthew 5:14-16.

18. A series of studies has been undertaken by the GEM global monitoring network in Richmond, VA, that provide a startling analysis of the effects of the unequal distribution of resources for mission.

19. John 4:1ff.

20. The Resolution of the Lambeth Conference of Bishops, July and August 1988 in Canterbury, England.

21. Bishop Yong Ping Chung of Sabah in the opening sermon delivered at the G-CODE 2000 Conference, Kanuga, NC, USA, September 4, 1995.

Chapter Three

1. John 17:1ff.

2. In John 17:21-22, Jesus prayed "that they may be one...that the world may see and believe."

3. Archbishop George Carey, speaking to the Joint Meeting of the Primates and the Anglican Consultative Council in Cape Town, South Africa, January 1993.

4. Missio Dei means Mission of God.

5. Lambeth Conference 1988, Resolution 43.

6. This point was raised more than once at the G-CODE 2000 gathering in North Carolina.

7. Galatians 4:19 (New International Version).

8. "People groups" is a widely used term in missiology to describe distinct human cultures. The following definition was framed by the Lausanne Committee for World Evangelization, and the AD 2000 and Beyond Movement, which is Lausanne's successor. "A people group is a significantly large sociological grouping of individuals who perceive themselves to have a common affinity with one another. From the viewpoint of evangelization this is the largest possible group within which the gospel can spread without encountering barriers of understanding and acceptance."

9. Matthew 10:37-38.

10. "The unsecularization of the world is one of the dominant social facts of life of the late 20th century." George Weisel, quoted by Samuel Huntingdon, *Foreign Affairs*, Summer 1994, p. 26.

Chapter Four

1. Hebrews 13:8.

2. The phrase, "The Hinge of History," was coined by Alvin Toffler in his book, Future Shock (London: The Bodley Head, 1970).

3. Eugene H. Peterson, "Spirit Quest," *Christianity Today*, November 8, 1993, pp. 27-28.

4. Roy Crowne of British Youth for Christ, speaking at the G-CODE Gathering.

5. Alister McGrath and Michael Green, *Springboard for Faith* (London: Hodder and Stoughton, 1994), pp. 108-111.

6. Ibid., p. 111

7. This evidence from China is beautifully explored by Nicholas D. Kristof and Sheryl WuDunn in their book *China Awakes!* (New York: Times Books, 1994).

8. *AD 2025 Global Monitor*, July/August 1995. Christian connection to the Internet had started to accelerate as 1995 ended, but there was still a long way to go.

9. "As they look to the future, teens see technology as one of the few unspoiled territories they may yet utilize to build a viable future. Where older people see

technology as a tool to be harnessed, teens view technology as a means of expression to be unleashed. In the battle for supremacy and authenticity, technology may prove to be the secret weapon of teenagers and their generation." George Barna, *Generation Next* (Ventura, CA: Regal Books, 1995), p. 115.

10. The Russian Ministry Network, which Richard Kew coordinates, is already committing to put significant numbers of computers into the hands of Christians in the Russian Orthodox Church.

11. Nick Cuthbert quoted by Nigel Scotland, *Charismatics and the Next Millennium* (London: Hodder and Stoughton, 1995), p. 249.

12. David Adams, *Powerlines* (London: SPCK, 1992), p. 98.

CHAPTER FIVE

1. This has been best defined by Loren Mead in his book, *The Once and Future Church*: "The (Christendom) paradigm's importance for us lies in the fact that most of the generation that now leads our churches grew up with it as a way of thinking about church and society. And all the structures and institutions that make up the churches and the infrastructure of religious life, from missionary societies to seminaries, from congregation life to denominational books of order and canons, are built on the presuppositions of the Christendom Paradigm — not the ancient, classical version of the paradigm as it was understood centuries ago, but the version that flourished with new life in the nineteenth and early twentieth centuries. This paradigm in its later years flourished and shaped us with new vigor, just as a dying pine is supposed to produce seed more vigorously as it senses the approach of its own death." Loren Mead, *The Once and Future Church* (Washington, DC: The Alban Institute, 1991), p. 18.

2. The Rev. Canon Michael Howard, Evangelism Advisor of the Diocese of Rochester, Kent, England.

3. "In order to be relevant to life and meet people's needs, theological education must address issues that concern all aspects of everyday life and worship — socially, spiritually, and materially." "Toward Dynamic Mission," The Anglican Communion Office, London, 1992, p. 36. Recognizing this problem, the Anglican Communion's Mission Issues Strategy and Advisory Group (MISAG II) in its concluding report, "Toward Dynamic Vision," which is now the working document for its successor body, Missio, suggested that mission should be made the fundamental basis for ministerial formation throughout the Communion.

4. The Rt. Rev. Benjamin Kwashi, Bishop of Jos, Nigeria.

5. As modest as the 1-1-3 approach seems, its long term potential is remarkable. A congregation of 50 would become 100 in three years, 200 in six years, and 400 in nine years. In just ten years those 50 Christians could, in theory, be turned into 500.

6. Acts 5:32.

7. "My tenure as a teenage leader convinced me that there is nothing like extensive involvement in youth ministry to motivate adults to give heartfelt thanks to God for allowing us to have survived the pain, the agony, and the frustrations of our teenage years so we could endure the mere tortures and headaches of adult life." George Barna, *Generation Next* (Venture, CA: Regal Books, 1995), p. 9.

8. Peter Ward, quoted by Roy Crowne of British Youth for Christ at the G-CODE 2000 Conference.

9. In 1995, in a presentation to a group of trustees and advisors of an Episcopal high school in the USA, a priest discouraged forthrightness about presenting the challenge of the Gospel to the students, basing his thesis upon data which was far from widely accepted even in the 1970s, when it was first published.

10. MTV is Music Television, a youth music channel now being seen around the world. It broadcasts both in English and Spanish, and will add other languages in the future. "Although there is no research to confirm it, MTV has probably had as great an influence on teenagers as any other television programming. The primary influence seems to have been the channel's ability to redefine teenagers' expectations of television programming, to reshape their attention spans, to present them with new ideas about society and relationships, and to confirm the acceptability of certain perspectives and behaviors." Barna, *Generation Next*, p. 53.

11. John Naisbitt, *Global Paradox* (New York: William Morrow & Co, 1994), p. 32.

12. Lamin Sanneh, *Translating the Message* (Maryknoll, NY: Orbis Books, 1989), p. 29.

13. Bernard Lewis, *Islam and the West* (New York: Oxford University Press, 1993), p. 42.

14. Bishop Kenneth Cragg speaking in a public lecture at Washington and Lee University, Lexington, VA, October 1994.

15. Archbishop Carey in an aside from the prepared text of the opening address to the G-CODE Gathering, September 1995.

16. Psalm 126.

CHAPTER SIX

1. This piece of evangelistic sharing is a cooperative effort of the Reformed Episcopal Church, the Diocese of Chile, and the British arm of the South American Missionary Society (Allen Gardiner House, Pembury Road, Tunbridge Wells, TN2 3QU. Phone: 0892 538647, Fax: 0892-525797).

2. Bishop Colin Bazley of Chile in a personal note to Richard Kew.

3. This is the U.S. arm of the South American Missionary Society (PO Box 399, Ambridge, PA 15003. Phone: (412) 266-0669, Fax: (412) 266-0297, E-Mail: 71303.1320@compuserve.com).

4. Central Tanganyika Press was founded on the initiative of Bishop Alf Stanway in the 1950s. It is one of the few Christian publishing houses whose sole commitment is the production of Swahili Christian literature. It is based on the outskirts of Tanzania's capital.

5. Romans 12:1-2.

6. Presidential Address, Synod of the Diocese of West Malaysia, 1994, p. 17.

CHAPTER SEVEN

1. Paul points up the gifts of the Holy Spirit in I Corinthians 12 and Ephesians 4. In Ephesians 4:11 he draws special attention to the spiritual gift of evangelism.

2. Evangelism Explosion is an approach to personal witness developed by the Revd. James Kennedy, long-time pastor of Coral Ridge Presbyterian Church, Fort Lauderdale, FL. It has been used in many countries around the world, and in the Anglican Church in Australia, Chile, and England, and it has yielded significant responses.

3. Paul told the jailer, "Believe in the Lord Jesus, and you will be saved, you and your household," (Acts 16:31). Household baptism appears to have been the practice resulting from a belief in, or assumption of household salvation. (Acts 16:14-15, 31-34; I Corinthians 1:16; Luke 19:9).

4. David Watson, *I Believe in Evangelism* (Grand Rapids, MI: William B. Eerdmans Publishing Co., 1976), p. 143.

5. Today there are Twelve Step programs dealing with everything from compulsive eating disorders to coping with every kind of sexual problem imaginable.

6. Robert B. Wuthnow, *Sharing the Journey* (New York: Free Press, 1994), p. 325.

7. Information shared with us by the Rev. Canon Ron Taylor, General Secretary of the New Zealand Board of Missions.

8. Acts 16:14.

9. Carl George, *The Coming Church Revolution* (Grand Rapids, MI: Fleming H. Revell, 1994), p. 26.

10. The Rev. Sam Shoemaker had extraordinary parish ministries in both New York City and Pittsburgh. With his wife, Helen, he established the Anglican Fellowship of Prayer more than 50 years ago.

11. Sam Shoemaker, quoted by George G. Hunter, III, *How to Reach Secular People* (Nashville, TN: Abingdon Press, 1992), p. 72.

12. Quote from a paper by Cyril Okorocha.

13. NAMS' target is 1,000 new congregations in its first 10 years in existence. It is backing up its ministry with an intense commitment to intercessory prayer and a call to repentance.

14. Nigel Scotland, *Charismatics and the Next Millennium* (London: Hodder and Stoughton, 1995), pp. 237-238.

15. These figures were taken from Robert Warren's *Signs of Life* (London: Church House Publishing, 1996), p. 44. *Signs of Life* is a mid-Decade of Evangelism review by the Church of England's Evangelism Officer.

16. George E. Barna, *The Frog in the Kettle* (Ventura, CA: Regal Books, 1991), pp. 28, 124.

17. The Episcopal Diocese of Milwaukee, USA, one of the pioneers of catechetical ministry, believes it will take a least a generation before the impact of their catechetical process begins to really work itself through the whole system.

18. Cyril Okorocha, *Christian Growth, Maturity, and Discipleship* (Owerri, Nigeria: Ihem Davis Press, 1987) has been reprinted a number of times and thousands of copies have been sold. It has helped those seeking after faith as well as those wanting to grow in their faith. Some parishes have used it in home groups; others have used it to assist with baptismal and confirmation preparation.

19. Marcia Brooks, quoted by Richard Kew and Roger White, *New Millennium, New Church* (Boston: Cowley, 1992), p. 57.

20. Warren, *Signs of Life*, pp. 83-84.

21. Frank Colquhoun, *Family Prayers* (London: SPCK Triangle, 1984), Prayer 115.

CHAPTER EIGHT

1. The term "convergence of saints" was first used to describe this phenomenon at the Three Rs Conference in Orlando, Florida, in January 1986, by the Rev. Dr. J.I. Packer of Regent College, Vancouver, BC, Canada. The Three Rs are Renaissance, Renewal and Reformation.

2. From the Foreword in *Charismatics and the Next Millennium*, by Nigel Scotland (London: Hodder and Stoughton, 1995).

3. Alister McGrath, *The Renewal of Anglicanism* (Harrisburg, PA: Morehouse Publishing, 1993), p. 6.

4. The message of personal holiness is a characteristic feature of genuine revival movements the world over.

5. Dr. Chinedu Nebo trained for ordination at ITAMA, a school of ministry that Cyril Okorocha directed in the 1980s. He is married, and he and his wife have three children.

6. EFAC in Nigeria is part of the worldwide network of evangelical Anglicans known as the Evangelical Fellowship of the Anglican Communion. The Rev. John R. W. Stott, Rector Emeritus, All Souls' Church, Langham Place, London, played a major role in the development of this network of evangelical Anglican Christians.

7. 2 Corinthians: 8,9.

8. Revelations 3:15-16 (Revised Standard Version)

9. Frank Colquhoun, *Prayers for Everyone* (London: SPCK Triangle, 1991), p. 114.

CHAPTER NINE

1. Archbishop Brian Davis, *The Way Ahead* (Christchurch, New Zealand: The Caxton Press, 1995), p. 137.

2. Lord and Lady Brentford are members of the Christian Parliamentary Fellowship in Britain. She spoke in North Carolina of the ministry of this group, and other Christians, among MPs and Peers in the British Parliament. Similar fellowships exist in conjunction with legislatures around the world.

3. Acts 4:31: "And when they had prayed, the place where they had gathered together was shaken; and they were filled with the Holy Spirit and spoke the word of God with boldness." (Revised Standard Version).

4. The following paragraph, taken from the prayer letter of an Anglican involved in planting a new congregation in Central Asia, illustrates the growing diversity of worship from their experience of the celebration of the Eucharist: "Though the 'liturgy' was similar to what you might experience in the west (i.e. including teaching on communion, reading from I Cor. 11, time of confession and preparation, etc.), some folks prayed in the Kazak (Muslim) fashion: prostrate. The bread was a special Kazak bread called 'shilpek,' eaten daily by traditional Kazaks. Following the final prayer, the Kazaks drew the palms of both hands down their faces (looks in a way as if they are wiping their faces with their hands), symbolizing the blessings of God being poured out. A bit different from what you'd see at an Episcopal church in the States, yet all of us share 'one Lord, one faith, one baptism, one God and Father of all.'"

5. John Sentamu is both a lawyer and theologian, and was formerly Chief Justice of Uganda. He is now a parish priest in London.

6. Helen Wangusa is a leading laywoman in the Church of Uganda, a member of the Mothers Union and the first Ugandan to be enrolled in the American order for laywomen, the Daughters of the King. She is the wife of a prominent Ugandan and the mother of a growing family.

7. At the first Anglican Encounter in the South at Limuru, Kenya, in February 1994, the question that echoed through presentations by clergy and laity, bishops and scholars alike, was, "Is it possible to be Anglican without adopting English culture and liturgy?"

8. This paragraph owes much to an article by Richard Kew and Roger White in *The Living Church*, January 5, 1996, and to the writings of the Rev. Linda Grenz.

9. Leighton Ford, *Transforming Leadership* (Downers Grove, IL: InterVarsity Press, 1991), p. 100.

10. Terry Fullam, quoted by Leighton Ford, *Leadership*, Winter 1984, p. 104.

11. Canon Michael Howard, Evangelism Advisor in the Diocese of Rochester, England, in a personal letter to Richard Kew, September 1995.

12. Canon Michael Howard, in his personal correspondence with Richard Kew.

13. Alister McGrath, *Evangelicalism and the Future of Christianity* (London: Hodder and Stoughton, 1994), p. 57.

14. From Archbishop Carey's opening address to the G-CODE 2000 Conference.

15. Alister McGrath, *Christianity Today*, June 19, 1995, p. 19.

16. Alister McGrath and Michael Green, *Springboard for Faith* (London: Hodder and Stoughton, 1994), p. 17.

17. Nicholas Gumbel, during a presentation in Fairfax, Virginia, quoted in *The Living Church*, October 1, 1995. More than 100,000 people participated in the Alpha Course in 1995 in Great Britain.

18. A very thorough and revealing examination of the emergence of AIDS and attempts to stem the flood of this appalling disease is to be found in Laurie Garrett's book, *The Coming Plague* (New York: Farrar, Straus and Giroux, 1994).

19. Archbishop Carey in his opening address at the G-CODE 2000 Conference.

20. Acts 1:8.

21. From the Profile of the Anglican Evangelistic Association of Tanzania.

22. During the last twenty years a network of independent, voluntary societies has come into being in the Episcopal Church, which has added new dynamic to the church's missionary ministry. Richard Kew has been deeply involved in this movement.

23. This happened through the ministry of the Russian Ministry Network of which Richard Kew is the Coordinator.

24. This is a dictum of Lyle Schaller, the Methodist Church consultant in the USA.

25. Douglas J. Elwood, "Riding the Third Wave," *International Bulletin of Missionary Research*, January 1992.

CHAPTER TEN

1. Ephesians 6:12.

2. I Samuel 17

3. Alister McGrath, *Evangelicalism and the Future of Christianity* (London: Hodder and Stoughton, 1994), p. 184.

4. Ibid, p. 64.

5. "The great movements of refugees and migrants are not just random occurrences in our modern world. We must interpret these massive and often tragic human dramas from God's perspective in Scripture... (giving us) permission to speculate why God is pouring people into the world's cities today. Are they only victims, or is God accomplishing something? I do not want this to sound like insensitivity to the plight which these people are suffering, but as Christian leaders we must think about them theologically as well." Ray Bakke, *Urban Christian* (Downers Grove, IL: InterVarsity Press, 1987), p. 82.

6. Alvin Vander Griend, quoted by C. Peter Wagner in *Churches That Pray* (Ventura, CA: Regal Books, 1993), p. 93.

7. C. Peter Wagner, *Churches That Pray*, p. 89.

8. Philippians 4:2.

9. Quoted by Todd M. Johnson in *AD2000 Monitor*, Number 14, December 1991.

CHAPTER ELEVEN

1. Quoted by Alister McGrath, *Evangelicalism and the Future of Christianity* (London: Hodder and Stoughton, 1994), p. 190.

2. *The Daily Telegraph*, 6 January 1996.

3. Ezekiel 37.

4. Douglas J. Elwood, "Riding the Third Wave," *International Bulletin of Missionary Research*, January 1992.

5. Quoted from Eucharistic Prayer C in *The Book of Common Prayer* of the Episcopal Church of the USA.

6. Revelation 7:9-17.

7. C. Peter Wagner, *Spreading the Fire* (Ventura, CA: Regal Books, 1994), pp. 69-70.

GENERAL THEOLOGICAL SEMINARY
NEW YORK

DATE DUE

			Printed in USA

HIGHSMITH #45230